BE RELENTLESSLY YOURSELF

BE RELENTLESSLY
YOURSELF

AND, TAKE ON LIFE!

EVELIEN VAN ES

Be Relentlessly Yourself is Evelien van Es's first edition

The author, the publisher and other parties involved in this book are in no way responsible and accept no liability whatsoever for any consequences arising from the use or application of the information contained in this book, nor for damage resulting from the book's interpretation. The reader is responsible for assessing the usefulness of the information and for its translation to their own personal situation.

Motivation Champs Publishing US
www.evelienvanes.com/en
www.relentlesslyyourself.com

First print 2021
© Evelien van Es, 2021

Isbn/ean book: 978-1-7354093-3-7
Isbn/ean e-book: 978-1-7354093-4-4
nur-code: 770/801

Proofreading and editing: *Bethany Votaw*
Design and layout: *Lynn Wagner*
Translation from Dutch: *Julie Kennedy*
Photography cover: *Herman Chow Portraits*
Publisher: *Motivation Champs Publishing*

The intellectual property and copyrights © pertaining to the content and cover of this book, belong to the author. Small quotations, with explicit reference to the source, are permitted. Subject to the exceptions laid down in or pursuant to the Copyright Act of 1912, no part of this publication may be reproduced, stored in a retrieval system, or transmitted in any form or by any means, be it electronic, mechanical, through photocopying, recording, or otherwise, without the prior written permission of the publisher or author.

TABLE OF CONTENTS

Introduction		7
PART 1	**REFLECTIONS**	**13**
1	A Reflection on Being Relentlessly Yourself	15
2	Eleven Souls, Eleven Reflections	27
PART 2	**LETTING GO OF WHAT HOLDS YOU BACK**	**73**
3	Making Room for Anger and Joy	75
4	Expressing Sadness and Acknowledging Fear	95
5	Letting Go of Expectations	111
6	Accepting What Is	119
7	Distancing Yourself from What Drains Your Zest for Life	131
PART 3	**GET TO KNOW YOURSELF BETTER**	**139**
8	Be Gentle with Yourself	141
9	A Healthy Ego	155
10	Distinguishing Truth from Reality	169
11	Getting Closer to Your True Self	179
12	Inner Growth	187
PART 4	**DEEPEN YOUR GROWTH**	**205**
13	Making Heartfelt Choices	207
14	Create Loving Relationships	219
15	Gain Energy Through Dreaming	231
16	Taking Up Your Own Space	239
17	Being Grateful	253
PART 5	**CONTRIBUTING**	**263**
18	Discovering Your Contribution to the Whole	265
19	Drafting Your Personal Manifesto	275
My Biography		281
Afterword		285
References		287

INTRODUCTION

Because nothing is permanent in life, almost anything is possible.

I am sitting in the garden under the bright blue sky. Not a single airplane stripe to be seen. Birds are chirping to their hearts content to my great pleasure, the purity of the sounds louder than ever. And to think that as a child I resented the bird's squabble waking me early every morning. Times change, but above all we do, as humans.

It is quiet outside and nature beckons. A large bumblebee flies by and lands in one of the plants next to me. I take the time to observe what is happening, how pollination takes place under my nose and I admire nature and her eternal cycle of life. The past few weeks have been brightened by abundant sunshine. A gift from Mother Nature which I believe is happening for a reason. As I write, the world is in the throes of the COVID-19 pandemic and going through strange times. People are confined at home and confronted with themselves. It affects us all, yet the contrast in how each individual experiences it, is great. I admire man's resilience, including that of my own children. Adolescents who want nothing more than to play sports with their team, to resume their social life. Worldwide we are all more or less in the same boat, and that connects us.

We tend to say: 'Rome wasn't built in a day' and yet, in times like these, you can see how a drastic change can occur in no time at all. How so many people suddenly slow down and take time for themselves, how creativity is unleashed, and people increasingly question what is really important to them in their work and in their lives. This movement is not new, we live in an era in which people are increasingly asking themselves: who am I really, what do I still want out of life, what do I want to leave behind and what have I done to date to accomplish that? This is about awakening.

The events of 2020 have accelerated the process, so that we are now moving from individual transformations and the broadening of our consciousness, to a collective change. This is cause for hope as this shift is badly needed. It is time to remember who we really are and to (re)discover our natural rhythm. Nature is our helping hand. Many people view nature as subordinate to us, I see it exactly the other way around. Nature's impact and power are tremendous, and it is times like these that help us to remember what is essential.

We are all part of these changes and have the choice to let it happen or even to play an active role in it. To create movement and turn the tide for the better. To choose not to settle any longer for a job that may bring in money but does not offer fulfilment. To end a collaboration or love affair because you feel that something essential, for you to be able to remain true to yourself, is missing which is just not possible in this context. To look for another place to live because you feel where you are is just not right. To find the courage to be *relentlessly yourself,* to express yourself and to set your boundaries. These are all choices we can make and make today. And even if some changes cannot happen overnight, we definitely can set them in motion. This requires your taking responsibility, facing up to what is really important to you. Are you prepared to make a stand for it? To continue to critically examine and question your purpose, to feel it, to look beyond your ego. To return to the core, to the essence, in connection with your soul, because that is where the source of our existence lies, and this is infinite.

Life Journey

So much for daydreaming in the garden. I am looking back at a truly special writing process, the birth of my book. I feel deeply grateful for the time and space I have been given to work on this book. To be able to inspire and encourage you to be yourself, to discover who you really are and have the courage to take on life. For me, this is where life's richness lies. To seek the deepest depths and not shy away from everything that is part of life and which makes it so valuable and exceptional. I would like to take you on this inner journey, because that is what it is.

Taking on life is all-embracing. It is about the light and the dark, everything that makes up our life journey. My life path so far has been a special but often intense journey, with beautiful, touching, warm and loving moments and also lessons and periods of sorrow and pain. My broadening self-awareness served as the foundation for me to see myself as I really am and to stand up for myself.

I wrote this book to encourage you, as a human being, a professional, and entrepreneur, to get to know yourself even better. To spark your curiosity about life and to discover what it really is all about. People are increasingly realizing that there is more to life and that each of us has the choice to fully live it or not. To trust and surrender to life. To truly discover who you are and dare to be relentlessly yourself. There are several key elements to this, which will be discussed in this book. These topics are common to all people to a greater or lesser extent and determine how happy and successful we feel in our work and in the rest of our lives. After all, success will never make us feel rich and fulfilled if it is without depth and meaning.

"Yesterday I was clever, so I wanted to change the world. Today I am wise, so I am changing myself." – **Rumi**

Book Structure

You will find a multitude of subjects in this book, though I do not claim to have covered everything. Allow yourself to be inspired and motivated to create your own picture and increase your self-awareness, in such a way that in the final section of the book you can draw up your personal manifesto, which can serve as a guideline in your work and in your life. You will find exercises in most chapters for which you can use the download at www.evelienvanes.com/download. Each chapter ends with a summary, for convenience sake.

In Part 1 you will read a variety of reflections on being relentlessly yourself and taking on life. In the first instance a reflection for you as a reader and then the personal stories and reflections of eleven extraordinary people around the world, that I interviewed on the theme of this book.

In Part 2, *Letting Go of What Holds You Back*, I will be taking an in-depth look at topics you will encounter on your way to being relentlessly yourself. Using examples and stories, I will examine emotions and feelings, such as the basic emotions of anger, joy, sadness, and fear. I will then move on to letting go of expectations, accepting what is and distancing yourself from what drains your zest for life.

Part 3, *Get to Know Yourself Better*, is about being gentle with yourself, about a healthy ego, about success and also about the difference between truth and reality. This part also deals with getting closer to your true self and inner growth in order to be who you are.

In Part 4, *Deepen Your Growth*, I talk about making heartfelt choices, creating loving relationships and how dreams and bliss bring you energy. I also talk about taking up your own space and the power of gratitude and of slowing down.

Part 5, *Contributing*, will discuss your contribution to the whole and I will conclude with the last chapter in which many of the topics come together to draw up your personal manifesto.

In this book I share people's stories in addition to my own insights: honest, personal, vulnerable, and pure. The stories in this book are based on true events and situations. The names of the people involved are fictitious in order to protect their privacy, with the exception of the eleven people I spoke to in Part 1.

Allow yourself to be taken on this inner journey, let yourself be moved and take action. I encourage you to give your voyage of discovery even more depth and meaning so that you can live your life the way your soul intends.

I wish you love, self-insight, and inspiration.

— *Evelien van Es*

PART 1
REFLECTIONS

1

A REFLECTION ON BEING RELENTLESSLY YOURSELF

"Anyone who chooses to take the path within, will experience loss. There is a false self that you have to free yourself from before you can shape the connection with your soul in your daily life. It is like breaking out of a cocoon." – **Pamela Kribbe**

To love someone yet choose for yourself because deep down inside you know you will lose yourself if you go on like this. To quit your job and jump into the deep, without knowing where it will take you. To speak from your heart to someone you love, sharing a rather tense but important message because it can be said. To feel pain and sorrow, and surrender to it, to experience your world collapsing for a moment, and then recover by (re)discovering confidence in yourself. To suddenly lose your job or assignment and see the free time offered as a gift. To cry, laugh, share, to speak out, to love intensely, to be deadly honest, passionate, to be relentlessly yourself, to make mistakes, choose for yourself at the risk of sometimes disappointing others, to set your limits, let others cross them and learn from it, that is what I mean by taking on life.

Life is about love, surrender and trust, has been my experience. To love with heart and *soul* and hereby dare be vulnerable. By *soul*, I mean the immaterial essence of a human being. It is about swimming on the waves of life, going with the flow, sometimes against a strong headwind, and sometimes even a raging storm. That is life, which at times can feel like an ordeal, depending on the experiences we have, the events on our path, the depths we plummet to. At the same time, it is precisely those depths that make us aware of the intensity of life. It is in fact nothing other than going through significant experiences on our life journey, so we can learn about ourselves and who we really are and what we are here to do. To take life for what it is. To live those experiences, that is what it's all about. You choose whether you dive into them and take them on, or flee for whatever reason you may have, as it seems too confrontational.

Each and every human being goes through significant experiences in life. Many carry old pain and sorrow that has accumulated as a result of traumas they have never really come to terms with. By traumas in this context, I mean the psychological impact of a situation you have experienced, of whatever order or size. It is not so much about the event, but the impact it has had on you.

You can only develop in life if you take on *everything*, the enjoyable and positive things as well as the pain, the sadness and by allowing yourself to make mistakes. If you were to brush away your past mistakes, you would remove the painful experience, but you would also lose all the valuable life lessons that have helped you become the person you are today. The inner wisdom you gain through all that you experience is priceless. We could also ask ourselves what mistakes are; mistakes do not exist, or merely in the perspective of the observer. More often than not, we ourselves are the critic, believing we should not be making mistakes. So, go ahead, and make as many mistakes as necessary, go and play, discover, take a few bumps and learn from them. That is how you get to know yourself. The biggest mistake you can make is to duck away and not work on yourself and your personal growth and development.

"In nature, if something is not growing it is atrophying. We are either developing or decaying. There is no interim stage. This is also true for our minds. When we are learning, we are growing and, literally, creating huge numbers of new brain cells. If we are stagnating, we are actually killing large numbers of brain cells."
– George Kohlrieser

We each have that choice and a great deal of influence over our lives, over how we live and how we perceive our life in terms of quality. This may seem like an open door, but in practice there are many who find the encouragement to really take on life, rather daunting. I understand, as it demands a lot of us and is not always pleasant in the moment. Nevertheless, running away is not the solution nor will it lead to fulfilment.

Surrender

I mentioned surrender as one of the core aspects of life. Life demands that you surrender, that you immerse yourself in it, that you at times feel you lose yourself only to find yourself again. It is only when you reconcile with the past and heal the pain of the experience, that you create the space to go on. You are then able to open your heart from a place of purity and experience beautiful new moments and fully enjoy them. Not healing that which has hurt you, will sooner or later inevitably lead to you bleeding on those who did not cause the bleeding.

In order to create space to experience new enjoyable moments, it is also important, alongside healing painful experiences, not to cling on too forcefully to the joyful moments that lie behind you. Otherwise, your current perception will be overshadowed by the past and will discolor the spectacles through which you see experiences and possibilities in the here and now. You probably recognize this in your surroundings or in yourself, people who regularly refer back to the past and relive and praise to the heaven's previous peak moments.

Looking back on beautiful memories is indeed wonderful and to sometimes have flashes of déjà vu with the things we experience is natural and should be enjoyed at that moment. The art is in letting the thoughts and beautiful memories emerge and let them go again in order to remain in the present moment. If not, you will only see the projection of the past memories, depriving yourself of the possibility of making new ones. It is in the now that we live.

Awareness as The Core of Your Being

We are on Earth, as human beings, to grow in consciousness. To become more and more aware of who we are. My awareness is the core of my being. Without awareness there is no living 'being' since there would be no awareness of it. The world around us constantly changes and we too evolve. Nothing is static. Just think of the brain cells. By developing myself in this life I create movement. I do this by unravelling who I am at my core, what I stand for, what my gift is and hence my life mission. I do so in such a way that I can put it in practice in this life. To unveil who I am, I need to take on life, to connect with people close to me, around me and also those far away. These are the mirrors that invite you to become aware of the subconscious and the unconscious and broaden your insights.

> Before moving on, I would like to take a moment to dwell on the distinction between the subconscious and the unconscious. Unconscious means not being aware and not remembering. Subconscious, on the other hand, actually means that you are aware, yet do not fully realize it. You could say that subconscious is between conscious and unconscious. Suppose for example, that you are driving home while talking to someone. It is getting dark and you know the way off the back of your hand. You know that feeling when you arrive home and are not aware how you got there? That is your subconscious. You know the way home, and your memory helps you get there without your being aware of it.

We each increase our consciousness at our own pace. If you choose not to deal with, then so be it. It is likely that the right moment for you will come when you are ready to learn and develop personally. It is not a competition; each being is here to grow. It is the ripening of your soul's development and your free will that determine the pace, and there is simply no right or wrong.

"Most people still identify themselves entirely with the ceaseless flow of the mind, of compulsive thinking, most of which is repetitive and meaningless. That is what being spiritually unconscious means." – **Eckhart Tolle**

Intelligence as recognized as social norm in society, has nothing to do with the development of your soul. The latter is about worldly wisdom and is acquired by going on an inner quest to the core of your being, your soul. This requires diligent work in order to confront yourself and your negative patterns.

Many people persist in their way of thinking and acting, and this hampers their personal development. We all do to some extent. The crucial element here is that you can only change and work on yourself when you feel an intrinsic driving force to take this on and refuse to stagnate. You recognize this feeling of stagnation for example by an underlying gnawing feeling of displeasure.

'Love is what lies at the end of our personal development,' notes the Swiss Christina von Dreien, who already at a young age was blessed with an unusually broad consciousness. Our evolution, our journey of the discovery of life, is fundamentally about love for ourselves, for life and everything that breathes and moves. When you stand on the threshold of your last moments here on Earth, love is all that remains, of that I am firmly convinced.

Being Relentlessly Yourself

Have you ever stopped to consider how unique a human life actually is? Merely the fact of being here on Earth, in this body, with this appearance and with everything you have in you, your gift to further develop yourself. I find it healing to sometimes stand still and feel profound gratitude for life and the uniqueness of this earthly existence. It enables me to sense how much greater our life is than we can comprehend and how much more meaning it enfolds than most of us are aware of. In essence, it is not about us as individuals, but about who we can be, how we can develop and what we can mean for the greater whole. By greater whole I mean society, nature, the Earth on which we cohabitate in order to be able to make that contribution.

In order to contribute to the bigger picture, we first need to focus on ourselves. That may sound like a contradiction, but I do not believe it is. It is only once we can see ourselves as we really are, that we can expand and use our gift, through our work and our lives for the good of the greater whole. The challenge is to do this from a place of purity and authenticity, and for that, we have to be ourselves.

There are two crucial aspects to fully embracing life:
1. *Take responsibility*
   When we take responsibility for being who we really are, we can serve the world with our unique talents and energy. This is only possible if our desire to serve is pure and brings us an inner sense of satisfaction and meaning. To get there we need life experiences to broaden our consciousness, to shape us and teach us lessons. It is often said that you are given what you can handle,

it is indeed so. Spiritual healer Jackie Freemantle aptly says: 'The brighter your light, the more darkness, hate, aggression or violence you can experience. Put a light on in a dark room and you can suddenly see everything.'

2. *Make an adventure of your life*
Enjoy life in spite of, and also thanks to the obstacles on your path. Even though the journey to our true self, to the core of our being, is not always easy, and sometimes even a real rollercoaster, life is not meant to be pure agony. Life is also about enjoying, feeling, and allowing lightness in, that is bliss. I feel that lightness as a sign I am in complete alignment with my soul. The playfulness, the naughtiness in me out are all part of who I am. My spice of life. When I am completely myself, I allow all of that to show, that is being relentlessly myself, without embarrassment. To act crazy, follow my heart, be unpredictable even though it may occasionally surprise those who do not know me well. In respect and with regards for my surroundings and the people around me.

This bliss is of course not a constant state of being, yet I find it an especially useful gauge of how I am doing. There are periods in my life when that being crazy and naughty fades into the background, then I am aware of it and remind myself that my life here on Earth may also be full of joy.

Remind yourself, despite the challenges you are confronted with – however intense they may be – that it is a privilege to live and enjoy the special moments you experience to the fullest. That joy can be found in the smallest of things: a kind message from a friend, a handwritten letter, someone saying he thinks of you, a friendly smile from a passer-by, an unexpected hug from your child or being blown away in nature by the beauty and perfect cadence of two swans taking flight. Life is full of hidden treasures, though not everyone has the peace of mind to be aware and notice them. I find joy in life in the intense connection with myself and with the people I love. That is life's magic and now that I see, feel, and act on it, my life has totally changed. It requires a different way of thinking, learning to feel deeply, having confidence – no matter what – speaking out from your heart and acting in line with it.

"The seed of the good lies within the bad."
– Pamela Kribbe

It is from a place of misery you may be in that you can (re)discover joy and gratitude for the beautiful things in life and feel the wonder again. This makes every experience valuable and even if your mind says, 'I am not doing well', your heart knows that it is okay because you are purifying.
    Real healing is more than just polishing the surface. It is about showing courage, facing, and coping with 'it', whatever 'it' may be, and trusting your body and carrying the pain you experience. Sometimes the pain can intensify before gradually disappearing. If you aim to approach both the sunny and the shadow side of life in a positive way, there is no escaping the need to take a thorough look inside yourself. Should you fail to do so, then you will be literally closing yourself off, not only from the outside world, but above all from yourself. You can run as much as you want, but wherever you go, you take yourself with you. Fleeing

is never a solution; you can try, but the boomerang will always come back to you.

We all have the privilege of free choice in life. There is no one to tell you what you have to take on or not, it is all up to you. The principle of free choice however implies that you take the responsibility for your choice, for yourself and for the people close to you who are involved or affected by it.

When taking on life, it is important to take up space, to allow yourself to be who you are and to express that. Taking up space means that you stand your ground and come forward. That you be heard and do not shy away from what others think of what you say or do, that you trust yourself and sail your own course, without hiding behind others. When you act from a pure heart, there is no reason to hold back or fear the consequences. This requires you to be vulnerable and to trust that your resilience will be there when you need it, no matter what life throws at you. To be able to take up space, it is important that you fully accept yourself as you are and that requires ultimate self-love.

As the subject and title of this book emerged, so did the idea of talking to eleven people in the Netherlands and abroad about their experience with taking on life and being relentlessly yourself. Each one of them with a unique profile and a deeply rooted story that moves. This resulted in a wonderfully varied group; eleven souls, eleven reflections. Allow yourself to be carried along in their contemplations and personal stories about being relentlessly yourself and taking on life from different perspectives, in the hope that it will trigger your own thoughts. That you may pause for a moment and become aware of where and how you stand in life and whether maybe there are other paths you would want to explore. So that you can be increasingly you, discovering your authentic power of being and living life in the way it was intended for you.

- ∞ Taking on life is all-encompassing, in essence it is about love, surrender and trust.
- ∞ Your awareness is the core of your being.
- ∞ Being relentlessly yourself and approaching life head-on requires you take responsibility for being who you are. For this, you must first be able to see yourself as you really are.
- ∞ Darkness and light are part of life and go hand in hand. The darkness enables us to (re)discover the beautiful things in life and marvel at them.
- ∞ To be relentlessly yourself, you need to take up space.

2

ELEVEN SOULS, ELEVEN REFLECTIONS

During the spring and summer of 2020, I got to speak with eleven wonderful people who shared their insights and experience of taking on life and what being relentlessly themselves meant to them. These were at times live encounters and in other cases, due to distance or the prevailing restrictions related to the COVID-19 pandemic, online video conversations. Each one a beautiful and intense conversation and a real pleasure; deep, warm, connecting, vulnerable and at times also touching. I came across these people and their unique story at some point on my life journey. Men and women of different nationalities, and with different backgrounds and career paths. These stories create a mosaic of how people look at life and give it meaning. Enjoy the stories, the thoughts and reflections and be inspired to think about them for yourself. What associations do you make around taking on life? What is being relentlessly yourself to you? To what extent do you live your life the way you actually want to, deep down inside?

With particular thanks to Frank, Femke, Mirjam, Robert Junior, Dieta, Wietze, Julie, Willem, Annemarie, David and Johanna Maria, for the beautiful in-depth discussions and the connection we shared which I intensely enjoyed.

1 | **Frank Oddens**

I was in a religious movement that had something in mind for me

A man with a mission. Frank Oddens (52) is a multi-entrepreneur, co-founder of Young Chiefs and a former orthodox Christian leader. He guides future leaders to discover their soul's potential, so they can use it in organizations transiting towards more purpose. He also does voluntary work and supports refugees in Greece. Frank has lived in England for many years and is based in The Hague (the Netherlands).

'In my life, it is not that I just read a book and woke up.' Frank's decision to leave the Church and resign from his position as pastor was deep reaching. 'It has been a complex and gradual process that went way back. Back to my childhood where I witnessed exclusion by the church, that even affected my family to the core. That hurt a lot, yet I still became a missionary of the message.'

He spent forty-five years of his life in the service of an organization that required something of him. Part of which felt right, but there were also parts he did not relate to, but to which he always said yes and amen. 'When they said: "You must jump," I replied: "How high?" Instead of me actually asking myself: why am I doing this and what is the context? I had always lived within that line of thinking, until at some point in 2018 I strongly felt that I was not being true to myself.' This became increasingly clear to him through the process he underwent with the Ojibwa tribe in Michigan. There he learned what genuine 'truthfulness' is, and realized he was supporting things that had no connection at all to his soul. 'I realized that I could no longer recognize myself in an organization that was exclusive and that I felt was not truthful. I had to turn inwards, to separate the institution from the humanity, for me there was no longer a match and then you get conflict within your soul. That leads to tension and bodily disruption.' He was confronted with an emotional challenge: 'What do you want: to continue or follow your heart?'

Frank has had several moments in his life when he wondered: 'Whose life am I living?', 'Whose rules are these?' As a child, he was often aware of this. He went to church on Sundays and to youth work on Wednesdays and was confronted with a reality that did not feel right for him. 'I think back to the times when I would hang around in church buildings on Sundays, and sometimes even on Saturdays, all smartly dressed when what I really wanted was to go outside.' He asked himself: 'What am I doing here, why are we here?' He did not drink cola, coffee, tea and, as a (young) adult, alcohol and swearing was against all rules. 'I could also see that people were not worse from drinking a cup of tea.' All these moments made him think: 'I was living an institutionalized life, as a child and later as an adult. There was no life of my own. I was in a religious movement that had plans for me and wanted something from me.'

Don't Stop Thinking About Tomorrow

When you decide to say 'yes' to life, things come your way that bring acceleration and growth. It also means having the courage to take paths you have never travelled before.

'Sometimes you find yourself in situations and think: should I have done this? Ultimately, growth is about gaining new insights and converting them into a direction that is good for you and for the world. That is gaining wisdom, and you cannot do it without courage, because it would mean missing the turns where those experiences lie.' We are programmed to look ahead at 'what are the consequences?'. Relinquishing control is about daring to accept what you cannot see and being at peace with things being as they are, whether good or bad. 'For me, life is about taking it for what it is. Sadness, pain, and anger will come again, but so will the feeling of happiness. If you can accept the contradiction of things, then you can become grateful.'

'Being relentlessly yourself is a beautiful thought, which for me that is about being yourself, about authenticity from the heart.' For him this sometimes means not being yourself, out of love. That the heart says: 'You do not go first right now because there are interests that are bigger than yourself.' Because you have a family for example, or you are dedicated to an organization with an important and pure goal. 'If you work for a non-governmental organization and something extremely urgent has to happen, like right now on Lesbos, which affects no less than thirteen thousand people, then I will postpone my own holiday plans and not be myself right now.'

Frank says that moral considerations are important to him and that does not mean a binary choice for yourself. Otherwise, that would be selfishness and the delusion of the day. 'Don't stop thinking about tomorrow.' You also have to take on that pressure. For him, that is leading a pure life, and being yourself is actually beautiful enough. 'Relentlessly yourself also implies being yourself whatever the cost, and therefore not looking at what that better picture entails. Sometimes in life you have to make a sacrifice at the expense of being yourself.' He was stuck in a path that wasn't right for him, which he had to leave in order to remain true to himself. That also has a downside, in terms of the consequences. You have to weigh it all up. 'Sometimes, you will consider being possibly less relentlessly yourself because of the consequences, which can be huge.'

My Heart's Way

His background has also brought him much. 'When I look at Nietzsche's modernist philosophical question which asks, "Suppose you were allowed to live your life one more time, not knowing that you would sign up for it the moment you stepped into the boat again, would you do it?" My answer is "yes".' He owes where he is today to what he has been through. He is glad that he was able to make a choice for himself, 'that I was able to follow my heart.' Without this process, Frank would not have looked back on his life so far with such happiness. He is grateful, 'also for what I learned in the church and for the people who put time and energy into my adolescent behavior, who wanted to orient me.' That has brought him something in every sense of the word and he cannot simply ignore it.

Frank lives with a moral compass. 'I am good at feeling and seeing where something leads, especially with people.' That is why he knows what he's getting into, also from a business point of view. He is grateful for this. 'I was already giving speeches in front of a crowd when I was eight years old.' This helped him develop well socially, also from an intuitive point of view and in the considerations he makes. 'The bottom line was that the *narrative* I was following was not mine. I had to make the choice to walk the path of my heart. I feel that I have succeeded in doing so, while retaining the good things.'

2 | Femke de Vries

Living someone else's life is hard to keep up

As a former director Femke de Vries (48) works at &samhoud as a Managing Partner and is also an endowed professor at the University of Groningen. She worked for years as divisional director and secretary-director for DNB and as director for the AFM. At the beginning of 2018, she made what was for her an extraordinary and courageous career move from her management role at the AFM to the world of consultancy. Femke is passionate about behavioural change and writes columns for Het Financieele Dagblad (a Dutch financial newspaper).

Femke's first association with the concept of 'taking on life' is of a sort of struggle. Personally, she always considered what came her way and at the same time feels she has been in charge of her own choices. 'You can still be in control, even if something is not planned. You can transform each role into something that suits you, where your strength lies.' At DNB she had several roles, and sometimes was asked to take on a new role whereas she was not yet finished with something else. 'I embraced this, trusting that there was a reason for it.' In life, according to Femke, it is a matter of going with the flow, and checking in with yourself if it still feels good. 'In my own career I have had a few moments when I realized that I had ended up in a comfortable position. For the sake of my own development, it seemed better to do something else. I was motivated by the desire to be challenged and to discover whether I could be successful in a different environment.'

Femke sees making choices in life as 'finding the balance between head and heart, and in my experience, at the end of the day you cannot make these kinds of fundamental choices with your brain.' She can still remember being on the island Schiermonnikoog and cycling round and round trying to reach a decision on taking on a new role. 'There were arguments to stay and arguments to leave, I just could not decide. There was uncertainty in both choices, and I got completely stuck in rational considerations. In the end, you have to take the plunge and make a choice.' What she found the hardest was saying goodbye to people, 'that feeling that you are burning the ships behind you. I experienced that feeling at DNB and also at AFM, you get attached to people and that has nothing to do with reason. My experience is that your heart bleeds a little with every choice you make.'

'Life is a river, and you follow its path, sometimes you take a side branch, and you don't know what lies beyond the next bend. Most people do want to see what lies beyond the next bend. Personally, I like the fact that I don't know exactly what's coming next.' Things come your way and for Femke it is important that she can develop intellectually and come into her own. 'That I feel I can add something and can continue to learn. That involves facing a certain uncertainty and trusting that you will learn something if you take on something new. Also, that you abstain from feelings of regret'. She sees regretting your own career choices as meaningless. 'When you are facing difficulties, you can think: oh dear, what now? Or you can take control and think: how can I find my place here? Besides, no choice is forever. Doing something you are not good at can affect your self-confidence and moreover you lose valuable time.'

For herself, she thinks she should work more on dealing with her sense of duty in life. 'I like to work, and I work hard, and many people are constantly making demands on me. It is still sometimes challenging for me to not automatically give in to the needs of others.'

I Have an Independent Spirit

Femke is convinced that you can only hold your own by being relentlessly yourself. 'You can't keep up a role which isn't you in the long run. Be yourself, even if others don't like it or if they don't think it's good enough. It is not always easy. It means not conforming to the group, if it is not in line with who you are. Living someone else's life is hard to keep up.'

'Being myself comes naturally to me, I have quite an independent spirit, already had as a child.' Being relentlessly yourself certainly does not mean to her not relating to others and therefore not taking their feelings and opinions into consideration. 'For me it has everything to do with being independent of mind; this is what I have to offer, some things I can do well and others I cannot, and that is how it is. This is also linked with accepting yourself and your shortcomings.' She believes that you should always relate to others with respect. So, for her, this relentlessness is mainly in the relationship with yourself and 'not making concessions to who you are, if that means violating your own convictions.'

Femke is constantly solicited from all sides. Sometimes for an article, to speak somewhere, for anything and everything. It remains challenging for her to not always be able to meet the expectations of others. 'I find it difficult when people appeal to me and I have to disappoint them. I find saying 'no' hard. But if you do not guard your boundaries well, it is a case of false loyalty. You are then spending your scarce time on things you may not even be sure are worth it, and it is another evening out. A colleague of mine at DNB once said: "Nobody asks themselves later on if they have worked hard enough," and that is the truth of the matter. This is about choosing what is really important to you. I know a lot of people who find that difficult.' People make choices to maintain a certain position, or for future assignments or for their visibility. Whatever your considerations may be, Femke believes we are sometimes governed too much by the future. 'You can ask yourself how useful it is to anticipate so much, "if this happens... then it will be useful that that." You can also choose to just let things happen more.'

Mutual respect is so important to her that it sometimes comes at her own cost, in particular of her me-time. Even though she knows she doesn't have to justify the choices she makes to others. 'From a mindset point of view, I make a good job of relentlessly being myself, but I do sometimes still feel tension around choosing what is really important to me.'

3 | Mirjam van den Boezem-Wijffels

My high sensitivity led me to carry a lot for others

At first sight a grounded and practical woman, but as an intuitive & energetic transformer, master coach and shaman strongly connected to nature and the ancient wisdom of the indigenous people. Mirjam van den Boezem-Wijffels (48) grew up in a medical family, graduated as an engineer at Wageningen University. She worked as a Trainee & Talent Development Manager at ORMIT and then as an independent trainer-coach, before leaving the corporate world almost ten years ago, to follow the path of her soul.

Life for Mirjam is 'embracing everything that is, feeling and experiencing every part of you. Take on the triggers and rising emotions that come your way and learn to listen to your body.' That can be anger or irritation. 'Dominant men were a trigger for me, for example, I made myself small, due to fear from the past'.

You will have to face your 'darker' sides and those of life, in order to make your dreams come true. Life is not a straight path to your unique dream.' It is a road with peaks and valleys in which you live your life. 'If you don't, which is a choice, you will never bring out the best in you. The question then is, will you ever be able to live the most loving life?'

For years, she dealt with every trigger and only now does she feel how connected she is to the source, the light, the love within herself. It took years of tough confrontations, which she would have preferred not having to face. 'Each step healed a part of me, my patterns, and my physical issues.' Only now does she realize that it has not been in vain. 'My soul called me unconsciously, time and time again, to let go of my old patterns, to search for my true self, my strength and potential.' She is still triggered every day but can now look at them with so much more love. 'I don't have to criticize myself anymore, I'm allowed to make mistakes, it's not a pre-made whole, everything is good as it is.'

Mirjam feels free when she is allowed to live her life her way. 'We are constantly adapting to existing systems. I decided my path would take me out of all systems; the business world, the fixed patterns of the family system and of my own system.' She even stopped her current business, in search of her 'own authentic primal energy, the essence of life. I also call it finding the wisdom within. By feeling and embracing this energy, I can increasingly go with the flow of life, in a way that requires no energy, with little or no physical issues.' Only now can she really enjoy life. Before, she was constantly fighting against thoughts and patterns which kept her stuck and cost her tons of energy. 'I worked hard and helped others in order to be seen.'

Many people, particularly during periods like the COVID-19 pandemic, are suddenly forced to take an other look at themselves and to start living their lives differently. 'Sometimes people dare not look, afraid of the pain hiding behind. The ego in us wants to protect us from this pain, from the unknown change. But at the same time, our ego also keeps us away from the love within.' Mirjam's path was one of wanting to know where the pain literally and figuratively came from and 'finding the love in myself.

When I meet someone, who is very caught up in their ego or resisting, who is hurt and does not want to budge, I can look at them with compassion. By acknowledging it, you are already in loving connection and that is enough. Because ultimately that is what it's all about, being in loving connection with yourself, with the other and with the world.'

Your Inner Wisdom is Your Source

According to Mirjam, life is about being who you really are, without the embellishments, patterns, thoughts, and illusions that have formed you, for example, through traumas. To be allowed to be pure, authentic, vulnerable, and happy. Living your life in your unique way, no matter how weird someone else may think it is. 'Following the call of your soul and by doing that, encountering all kinds of things. Emotional ups and downs, periods of happiness and periods in which you no longer know who you are and what you are doing it for, such as my burn-out at the age of twenty-three.' Which she now knows, was caused by the learned behavior of constantly adapting to others and, 'given my high sensitivity, carrying a lot for others. I was not myself and my body literally stopped working.' The right side of her body was paralyzed from carrying the burden of others. 'It was intense, but I got out of it by changing my behavior. Your body knows that you are crossing the line and starts protesting. Your body is an intelligent instrument. But what do we then do? We go to a doctor and say, "I have pain, fix it." Whereas the real solution lies mostly within us.'

In her life, it was mainly during the moments in nature, in Africa as a child, in Costa Rica during her studies and later with her family in Australia, and the journeys she made with her clients, when she felt good and was completely herself. 'I then felt a primal energy, a pure surge of happiness and joy and a tremendous connection with nature and the people around me. Then I felt at home!' Unfortunately, she often lost that feeling within a day of returning home. She later realized that it had to do with the old fixed systems she returned to where she, of her own choice, adapted again to what she thought was expected of her. 'I went through many grueling periods to learn my lessons. I often felt worn out by the physically demanding ordeal. My body took it all on.'

Mirjam is now in a phase leading her she does not yet know where, and she accepts it as she trusts this is happening for a reason. It is for her, a phase of surrender, of letting things happen and doing what feels right. 'I am allowed to enjoy myself and it is important I be grounded in my body. Only recently did I realize that it is a game between your soul, your heart, and your ego. Which part is my soul, what does my heart desire and what is ego?' She has pursued several desires, and in retrospect she can see that some of them were directed at old pains, desires of her ego, 'collective thoughts on when you are a successful person. They are often not real.' So, she wanted to contribute to healing the world we live in and helped everyone by healing them, without listening to her own limits. 'Now I know that this was fed by the pain of wanting to save lives, I thought I was being a good person in doing so. The lesson I was allowed to learn is that I only need to be myself. The peace, the love that you feel in yourself radiates out. Everything is energy and your energy or vibration influences your surroundings.

It is important to be aware of this. Each time you become aware of something, you enter a new level of consciousness, with a higher and lighter vibration. Each step brings us closer to a new life we could not rationally have imagined possible.'

There is no room for doubt when she feels totally connected to her base, her belly, to her heart and soul. 'My body knows what is good for me and what is not, and what makes me happy. Your inner wisdom is your source! You then do exactly what you were meant to do in this world at this moment, whatever it may be. We do not know how wise we are and are invited to discover it for ourselves. You cannot come to terms with that with your head. To have faith in the deep wisdom within, to be a true master and your own leader, then you will live your life.

4 | **Robert Harper Junior**

Colleagues of mine had jumped out of those buildings

He is a filmmaker, producer, model and passionate environmentalist based in the New York area. Robert Harper Jr. (52) is originally from the USA but grew up in Germany. He is an alumnus of Brown University, Digital Film Academy and studied at Harvard Business School. RJ worked with Goldman Sachs on Wall Street. A spiritual soul with roots in Nigeria and Native America that shares my passion for sungazing and the water.

He was pursuing his banking career, as a black male in America on Wall Street, trying to do all these great things in the corporate world. It was living a life of external success and then the 9/11 World Trade Center was bombed. 'I was there at the time, in the lobby of the burning building. I have never been so conscious of the fleetingness of life than when I was trying to get out of that building.' When he eventually got out and ended up in the hospital, he realized that so many people had died. He had an epiphany and realized that life is very short and that he had been given another chance. 'And if you're going to live your life, do the things that you love and feel passionate about!'

Actually, RJ feels that he shouldn't be here, physically, 'but the universe tells me that I'm supposed to be here.' He is here to use the time that he has in ways that completely changed the direction of his life. 'With that I've become a more grounded spiritual person. Not religious necessarily, but me getting the time to get to know myself as a person. What is this human body that I have, how connected am I to my own self?' For him this is understanding your own energy, your *chakra zones* and how to align yourself to connect with the larger energies of the universe.

He had some big questions about the universe after what had happened, 'I had time to ponder and felt depressed.' Trying to find a path forward, required some inner soul-searching on what he wanted to do. 'I had been accomplished, been to Harvard, worked on Wall street seventy hours a week, traveling everywhere. I was on the right path to be a successful guy by American standards.' However, he felt like he didn't know himself, 'so I had to take some action.' He started scuba diving and yoga and went back to film school, something he was very passionate about. He became a rescue scuba diver and won the Guinness book of world records by organizing the largest underwater clean up in the history of the world. It brought together over six hundred professional divers from around the world who wanted to make a statement about how mankind is ruining our planet with ocean pollution. 'That was very fulfilling.'

Don't Let Others Dim Your Light

'I need to remind myself how important it is not to dim my light sometimes, in order to accommodate other people.' Life changing experiences make you appreciate the extent to which life is somewhat fleeting, says RJ. 'How do you use your energy when you really come into your own power in a way that you understand who you are?' For people who get it, it turns into a spiritual journey that takes you out and away from other people who are just on their way to get a check, to get a job and do their career.

There is a spiritual awakening that comes from living life but also having experiences that require you to tune into the larger universe. 'What is it that you're doing here, what is your purpose for being here? Understanding who you are as an energy source on this spinning rock that is going through space at 10.000 miles per hour. How do you contextualize that and find a way to make sense of life?'

If you are going to be on this planet and if you have some sense of your own presence here, regardless of any forces coming your way, then own your inner power. 'My spiritual journey to understand who I am also brought me to do my (African) DNA-test. To find out who I'm connected to and that was mind blowing. Besides being 10% British and also Native American, I found out that I have tribal roots that extend to the monarchy of the Nigeria Edo-tribe which brought about a broad spiritual awakening in me.' If he had never done that, he would have been a very disconnected person from who he is now. 'I found the link for my passion for water in my roots in Nigeria and that means a lot to me.'

Sungazing is his way of charging his battery. 'When I sun gaze, I give my entire soul an opportunity to absorb as much energy as possible from the sun.' If you're connected to the idea that you're trying to recharge your battery, you know the value that sungazing has.' 85% of the people on the planet just don't get it, 'I think that is a tragedy. I don't want to go through life and leave this planet with a lot of questions, on who we are and what we are supposed to be and what this planet is all about.' Some of the answers are right here for us, if we take the time to listen to the Earth, to mother nature, to the universe and take the time to just ponder the sun. Many people are stuck on their treadmill of 'just doing things'. 'It's the spiritual journey that I think is so crucial. That you realize that once you're in your power, you can be such a powerful light being and light bearer.'

I'm in My Third Life Now

RJ thinks he is in his third life within this life by now. 'In your life before your awakening, you're not focusing on any type of development besides the typical career stuff. You're a go getter, over achiever, focusing on winning.' He always wanted to come home with the trophy, 'it was my way to get love and attention from my father.' When you own your own power, you realize it's not really you and that it doesn't work. 'I don't have to win at everything.' Getting out of that bubble was very important for him. After 9/11, he realized how blind he had been. 'Colleagues of mine had jumped out of those buildings. I was completely at a loss to what that person's life then meant. They achieved everything to get to that corner glass office and then one day you wake up with all those achievements and your life choice is now either to jump out the World Trade Center or get caught in the flames.' He thought: 'This is not the way to go. That person probably never wanted that job in the first place but did it to make money and then finally do what they really wanted.'

He took the time to try and heal by seeing a psychiatrist. 'Trying to navigate life after some kind of traumatic experience can be very tough. We live in a society that tells men to power through this, to get over it.' RJ thinks life is great as he has been able to come through on some things and it allowed him to stand in his own power and he can be vulnerable. 'I'm a voice, a non-traditional voice about some of these things.'

So many people haven't found their own path in life, he says. Every individual should do their DNA-test. 'It would likely end racism immediately when we wake up to the fact that we all are such a mosaic of so many different cultures.' And it also opens up the possibility to align with your spiritual nature that you might not be aware of now. You sometimes deny things that the universe is trying to tell you and that you should awaken within yourself. 'Society doesn't allow us to get off the treadmill, but COVID-19 is slowing people down, making them take time out and reconsider their career options. I heard someone call covid an autoimmune respond from mother earth. The planet will look out for itself.'

5 | **Dieta Brandsma**

Dealing with life and death daily

Every day she deals with patients confronted with life and death. Dieta Brandsma (49) is a medical specialist attached to the Antoni van Leeuwenhoek/Netherlands Cancer Institute in Amsterdam. As a neurologist, she specializes in brain tumors. In 2020, she appeared in a Dutch TV program Over mijn lijk (Over my dead body), on young people who are terminally ill. In her spare time, Dieta is a keen cyclist.

She is often confronted with life on a professional level and also with how you deal with an approaching death. 'You can't know in advance how you will feel once the end of your life is in sight, unless it actually happens to you. I have never felt that I was not taking on life.' She does not worry much about practical matters. Dieta thinks there is a solution to many practical matters, or you just say to yourself 'it doesn't really matter.' She thinks that this ability to put things into perspective is thanks to her work, in combination of course with her nature. 'As a child I was already serious and driven, admittedly with a sense of humor and the ability to put things into perspective. In my student days that ability increased even more.' Initially, as a medical biologist, she wanted to focus solely on scientific research. But she also really enjoys the social aspect of life, people and how you can help others. That led her to become a medical doctor as well as a medical biologist.

'Life, for me, is about deciding for myself how I want to live my life.' She comments on how this can be different at various stages of your life. Taking care of your parents is not usually on the agenda before you turn forty, but after it might be. This has a big impact on your life. But also, whether you live alone or have a partner. That also has an influence on how you stand in life and live it. For me, taking on life also means not avoiding difficult conversations, socially speaking, however difficult that may be at times.'

Feasibility of Being Relentlessly Yourself

When talking about being 'relentlessly yourself,' Dieta admits struggling with the word relentless. 'I believe in being yourself, but I don't think that being relentless in it, is always a good thing.' In society, in social life and in work, we are always in relation to others. 'It is not always a good thing to be relentlessly yourself as there are consequences for you, for others and because it can also damage relationships.'

She feels that in her private life, in her relationship, she can be completely herself; she feels no inhibition, or almost none. 'Things are slightly different within family relationships.' She sees it as more complex because how you were raised, educated, and also the social context which formed you will also come into play. 'This is something you will always have to deal with, you are always confronted with how you are in relation to others.'

In our professional life, we have a certain role. People have certain expectations of her as medical specialist. 'You can be your own person in that role, and it is also important that you do so, albeit in an appropriate way.' For her, this means assessing the extent to which this is possible and desirable within a doctor-patient relationship. 'If I stay close to myself, that means bringing a combination of empathy, honesty and information on the basis of substantive knowledge.' Dieta shares that patients' questions are sometimes very surprising and of a completely different nature than you would sometimes expect, 'you have to respond to that and in that you bring your true you.'

A Matter of Life and Death

She deals in her work with life and death on a daily basis. With an approaching death and the choices that have to be made in terms of treatment, or non-treatment, and what this means for someone in the last phase of their life. 'I see that as part of my work. What can move me is the involvement that I see in loved ones. By this I mean the reciprocated love for the patient. That sorrow has impact and affects you.' Welling up at work is not a problem, but she is well aware that it is not about her. 'With some patients you have built up a long-term relationship, so it doesn't matter if the medical team is also affected.' But she finds bursting into tears herself not very functional, and that means to her, it is better not to be relentlessly herself in situations such as these.

'I am part of a generation that believes that everything needs to be dealt with or discussed'. She thinks that is a good thing, when compared to 'our' parents' generation or earlier. That there is openness and more discussion with each other. 'But I do not think you need an outlet for everything, or at least that's how I see it. I am less in need of some things, such as exposing our vulnerability. But then again, we are all different.'

6 | **Wietze Reehoorn**

Not running away from the confrontation with yourself

He worked at ABN-AMRO *for no less than thirty years, eight of which as a member of the Board of Directors. Wietze Reehoorn (58) does not sit still. He is currently both a Director of the National Bank of Greece and Chairman of the Supervisory Board of* MUFG *Bank Europe and advises an international family business. Wietze combines this with five additional supervisory roles at social-cultural organizations in the Netherlands. Wietze loves the sea and plays the piano with considerable skill.*

In 2018, after a thirty-year career with ABN-AMRO, he wanted to be free and job-less for a while. 'I needed that freedom in order to be able to feel and rediscover who I am.' He took that time, which was about a year and a half. 'A lot came my way, but I pushed it all away. It felt curious, but above all, it felt good'. People around him said: 'You've got such a track record, you have it all for the taking, why not do it?' But he did not do it, because he wanted to 'feel life in absolutely everything.'

In his last eight years on the Executive Board, Wietze realized how much it demanded of him. 'Even though I am at my best when a lot is going on, you end up living and thus enjoying less. I live close to the beach but had stopped going there. The busy job takes all your time, and you end up letting go of the rest.' Once he had left, he needed the freedom in order to be able to fully feel himself. 'I went to the island of Texel on my own, twice. I was really faced with myself; anger, frustration about everything and anything came out.' He also felt gratitude for what he had achieved: 'a beautiful family, a great career, no financial worries and a great circle of friends.' There on Texel, he very consciously took it all on. For him, that is what embracing life is all about, not shying away from things. He needed to do that alone. 'The sea has a healing effect on me, I can look at it for hours, and I also love it when it is stormy. I kept myself free from work because I wanted to deeply feel what life then brings.'

During this time of reflection, Wietze also asked himself: 'What do I want to do with the next thirty years? How do I want to go about it and what can I do to be happier?' He says he has lived a grand and exciting life and there has always been a lot going on. 'I have done a lot, both professionally and privately. I have worked hard and travelled a lot with my family and lived intensely.' That is how he wants it. He feels that he has become freer and lighter in his life, but in a nice way. 'It's not in my system to slow down, I still want to experience things in life. I feel full of energy, I can still do a lot and I also would like to contribute, to help others and learn and grow myself. If you open yourself up to it, it will come your way, and so it did.'

What he finds important in life is not to run away from the confrontation with yourself. 'Let it be uncomfortable for a while.' Beautiful things can emerge from chaos. 'I have gradually come to realize and feel that you cannot influence everything in life. A kind of Taoist peace has come over me with the thought that if something is as it is, then it is meant to be.' There can also be acceptance when something doesn't feel right, and you know you have done everything you can.

He has a certain hunger and curiosity to live life. 'I have so many encounters with people, beautiful contacts that come out of it.' He experiences it as being much more open to life. 'I also hear and see nature better, I paint nature much better and I play the piano a lot.'

Self-leadership

It is important to Wietze to have the space to be who he is, 'so that it can flow.' For him, being relentlessly yourself is above all 'being true to yourself and being authentic,' which he does as much as possible. 'I want to have contact with people, it makes me feel good. Being playful, occasionally crazy, also in my work, that's who I am.' He loves being able to set his own agenda in his work, that is what he wanted. At the moment he has eight different roles in parallel, 'that's a bit much, but I decide myself now.' As a banker, he now stands with one foot in – what he considers – the 'old familiar world' and with the other in a completely new one. Working with Greek and Japanese culture is really different for him, as is working in an international family business. He does all this alongside his pro bono social roles in the Netherlands.

'I am very loyal, and I do not give up easily. That is sometimes a good thing and sometimes not.' At times, this is at the expense of being true to yourself, Wietze believes. 'I still occasionally have the tendency to carry someone else's suitcase. This can be good, but there are moments when it is better not to, and to leave it with the other person. I am now busy with self-leadership. Leading myself is a lot more complicated than anything else I have done. You are yourself and that takes courage.' The impact of those around you is great. He believes that wanting to be good to everyone, to be loyal, can sometimes get in the way of being relentlessly yourself. 'To be deeply engaged in what moves you and how you want to move forward in life makes me feel good, and I do it my way.'

7 | Julie Kennedy

I want to live a life of no regrets

She calls herself a nomad and a 'free spirit' and has moved twenty-two times to date in her life. Julie Kennedy (53) is a communication specialist, translator, editor, and life coach. She is British and lives in a lovely spot on the Dutch coast. As a child and later as partner of a diplomat, she lived abroad for years, including ten years in Africa. What many people do not know about her is that she is a Nichiren Buddhist.

Moving so often in her life has become part of who she is. 'Even as a child, I think I had moved thirteen times by the age of seven.' When she was born in the summer of '67, her parents were only nineteen and still studying. She spent her first year with her paternal grandparents in Ireland because her parents went abroad for their studies. 'When they returned, I went through everything with them, graduation, their first job, including being literally "hidden in the closet" when the landlord passed by. I think this *bohemian* start of my life also contributed to the perception that my life is an adventure.'

Julie explains how her life has actually been a nomadic existence. Her own children grew up in Cameroon, Uganda, and Senegal. 'For me, home is where I am, the people I meet, and what I have made of it.'

Having moved so much, sometimes makes her feel a bit lost. She has British nationality but has actually only lived a very short period in Britain. 'First my parents decided where I lived, then my former husband and then I did what was best for the children.' Now, for the first time in her life, she gets to decide where to make her home. 'The idea of maybe staying in one place forever scares me. I have learned so much from all the people and cultures in the different countries I have lived in, and it has enriched my life so much. My horizon has constantly expanded.' This has created a strong desire for variety which suits her tremendous amount of energy. 'I throw myself wholeheartedly into everything I believe in and I give it my all.' She says 'yes' to almost everything in life, goes full speed and wants to get the maximum out of it. 'This sometimes makes me feel that I have already lived nine lives so far. It is intense, it is accepting what is and moving on with what you have learned.' She is powered by resilience. Life for her is all-encompassing and the most sacred thing there is. 'Learning from the past, making plans for the future, but living in the now. That is not holding back and waiting for a better day, not thinking that I will be happy and fulfilled once I have my car, my ideal job and life partner, but what can I do to be a better person today than I was yesterday.'

Embracing Life

Julie embraces life, does her best not to judge, not to compare, but to live her own life. She is more interested in 'being' than 'doing.' She believes in not letting your experiences determine your life but detaching yourself from them. 'There will always be things which trigger you in life, we cannot control what comes our way, but we can influence how we react.'

Age works in our favor and 'fortunately I am blessed with a sense of humor. I can experience huge ups and downs, but humor helps me bring lightness back. It is living through the pain that makes you stronger.' That has made her a person with compassion and understanding for what is really important in life. 'There can be no light without darkness, and I know that the darkness will always be part of my life.'

Aged fourteen, she moved from France to the Netherlands. 'I went to the French Lycée of The Hague. I was rather rebellious and was therefore sent to boarding school in France for a year.' Those were crazy years for her, surrounded by sons of French African dictators, but also children who were in social care. It was a vastly different environment, another adventure that shaped her. 'I have had wild years, done and discovered all sorts of things.

Once I went to university, I developed a taste for learning and have never managed to stop.'

She has felt all her life that she had to prove herself and craves recognition. 'It was never enough. My name "Kennedy" probably also plays a role in this, taking responsibility, leading. It created the image of who I have become.' She often felt different and that the expectations of those around her were high, 'or maybe they were mine.' She used to have to be 'President' of everything, now she withdraws more often. 'I live close to the sea and that is a wonderful place for me to live and be and to come to myself. When I feel lost, when I no longer know who I am, what I believe in or what I feel, then I let the grandeur of nature bring me to rest. Then I am better able to put my ego aside and feel how I am one with the universe.'

She is not afraid to fail and believes everything happens for a reason. If you fall, then you have the opportunity to learn and emerge stronger. 'I do not want to have regret for not doing things.'

Accepting Who I Am

For her, relentlessly yourself is being that generous, vibrant, loving, and caring woman who is determined to make the world a better place. 'I believe that happiness lies in an authentic connection with ourselves and with others.'

Julie does a lot for other people as she believes that that is where true happiness lies as a human being, but she has largely let go of the expectations of others. In order to stay true to herself, she needs time for herself, 'to meditate, do yoga, Pilates, and *chant* and thereby tune in with my body and my *inner Buddha*, full of love, compassion and respect for the value of every other human being.'

One of the challenges she faces is her inner conflict between the urge for freedom and at the same time for stability, security in her life. 'In my life I have been on the move, done, seen, and experienced so much, that that sometimes make me find it hard to feel at home.' Now that her children have left home, she is looking for more stability in her life.

'In order to accept yourself as you are, it is important to be able to laugh at the things you are less good at. First you need to understand yourself as a human.' She has a positive view of humankind and does not believe that there are bad people, 'only people who have had bad experiences. I try to see the good in other people's bad actions. Each human being is responsible for their own life, for the things that happen and the decisions that we make in consequence.'

8 | **Willem Smit**

I have had to learn to enjoy who I am

As a poet and artist, he cannot be summed up in a few words. Willem Smit (29) is an intriguing and self-confident man, introverted in character and at first glance an old soul in a young body. An artist of the word who lets himself be guided by imagination, inspiration, and his love of language. He is amongst other things the Rabobank's in-house poet and works as a language artist.

Willem grew up in a fairly Calvinistic family as the eldest of five children, with a pastor as father. 'There was not always room in this family environment for great things at an individual level, such as having a rich and creative mind. The group, duty, the old stories, proving oneself useful, are what set the tone.' He did not easily fit in the system. He sees this as 'one of the flaws of the performance society we live in. It is important that you get the right diplomas and are a respectable, productive citizen with a congruent story, but what if you can't, or can't be pigeon-holed?'

'Life, in the end is about fully embracing your greatness as well as your fragility.' This is something he has had to learn. According to Willem, confronting fragility is not an easy task. 'We live in a society of arithmeticians, know-it-all's and risk controllers, with organizations full of valiant professionals and streamlined processes, and there is not always room for things that go beyond that.' For example, not knowing. Many try to radiate the opposite: 'You have a life plan; you have your career all mapped out for the next five to seven years. You are "in control". People trust you when you come up with the answers and this makes it hard to let go of that.' It makes him feel uncomfortable at times, that this could be mistakenly interpreted in society's eyes as a form of unwelcome 'fragility.'

He emphasizes that 'the core story of the Christian faith acquires a special eloquence against this backdrop. Believing, in a broader sense of the word, is having a hopeful, spacious relationship to both greatness and fragility. The fragility of the figure of Christ, in which the weak at the end turn out to be powerful and uplifting.' He sees this as a paradoxical story that does justice to how people are, to how life is. 'It would be wonderful if more people discovered the greatness that resides in not knowing and in impasses. Cathartic lethargy, salutary dysfunction and underachievement.'

He also encountered this in his youth. He needed a lot of space to process stimuli and had a rich inner life and a great imagination. This in an atmosphere where it was not always understood or recognized by others, 'which made me bottle it up. The tendency was often: "Just act normal, that is already crazy enough", based on the idea that there are bigger things than you, namely the divine, the community, morality.' Fortunately, in the meantime he also met people who took it a step deeper. 'All in all, this climate provided me with beautiful blocks to build on and I am happy with my roots. We live in a time of immoderation, a time when anything goes. Thanks to my upbringing, I am not averse to moderation and self-control, although I can sometimes go a bit far in that respect. I have really had to learn to enjoy who I am, the beautiful sides, but also the frayed edges.'

Discovering, in the Void, How you Want to Live

He is more about 'living in the spirit and less about living by the letter.' By cutting loose from his parents and the pillar from which he came, he could discover in the void how he wanted to live, how to fill his days and who he wanted to gather around him. 'I had to figure out who I am. There where I used to learn to integrate, I started to disintegrate. I started to periodically reject norms, the group and the system; the society that we had established together.' He lived for a long time in a sort of vacuum, started things and stopped again, led a somewhat chaotic and erratic existence. 'All in all, it brought me a lot. A sense of freedom I had not known, and also the feeling of surprise at the twists and turns of life.' Gradually, he rediscovered that to be creative, he also needed 'the peace, purity and regularity of the old days.'

That disconnection also helped him to develop a certain 'quirky behavior' and to tap into it himself. 'This too is who I am. Verbally I always was, but I then also started internalizing it in terms of lifestyle.' He enjoyed the chaos, but it also gave him a sense of insecurity and 'the question is whether I profoundly enjoyed it. You can enjoy grandly from your ego; the question is whether that is a deep-seated enjoyment or the ego speaking.' He says he has a thing with virtue, but just as much with vice. 'I like impossible behavior and I was not easy on myself or on those around me. I was outspoken, said what I thought. I was not calculating and did not want to be everyone's friend. Daring to be inappropriate is your downfall as everyone's friend.'

Freedom of Thought and Speech

Freedom of thought and speech is important to Willem. 'Maybe that has something to do with the past, when I didn't always feel there was this sanctuary.' He gets on well with people he can be open with, without them keeling over or seeing it as an ego battle.

To be free without a permanent job is what he likes about living life in his own way. 'Riding my natural waves of inspiration, setting my own pace.' It keeps him sharp and awake. However, the freedom can be overwhelming, and he can drown in it. 'I always have excess capacity, in energy, ideas, words and insights. It can't all lead somewhere.'

Simplicity helps, starting the day with pen and paper, writing poems. 'Calming your mind. Something new may arise in the calm, an insight, a word, or a discovered connection. All these thoughts and emotions of mine are great forces that sometimes need to be able to smash against a rock. If I don't, it can also smash on the inside.'

When he no longer writes and speaks, the latent present in him starts to nag a little. 'In order to feel grounded and vital, I sometimes have to express with great force what is important to me and what resides within me. Putting this into words can be such a relief. Language is incredibly powerful; if you find the right word at the right time, then what is spoken or written literally and figuratively gains strength.'

Willem finds it beautiful when language touches the heart and creates movement, he calls it 'life-giving language'. He takes pleasure in writing something that makes readers think: I am being kissed awake again, or: I feel understood again. 'Writing something that people can get up with and go to bed with. Something that helps them look death in the eye, but also life. Something timeless.' He does not need to be famous when he is gone. He wants to feel that something has quality. 'Texts that do justice to the paradoxical and mysterious nature of existence, in form and content.'

He has no fears when it comes to life and death. 'I have got used to dying in life itself, that gives me courage. My feel for life is the attitude that life is not always a party. It is a real awareness. Sometimes you have to go through despair to gain hope again.'

9 | **Annemarie Geysen**

To become and be an old and wise woman

She studied social psychology, did an MBA, and sat on both sides of the table as consultant and HR director of an international construction company. Annemarie Geysen (50) is founder and consultant at STYR, a scale-up management consultancy with an innovative and 'fair' remuneration model. Her heart lies with pragmatic, innovative (family) businesses in the technical, maritime, and offshore sectors. She is from Zeeland, loves the water and the wind, and at weekends can preferably be found on a boat on the Gouwzee and the Markermeer.

When she was in her late twenties, she went from being an HR advisor to a consultant with an American consulting firm. 'I had created an image of myself as a typical business minded consultant, partly inspired by all the professionals around me. I tried extremely hard to be that type of consultant. It was a total failure.'

By nature, she makes informal contact with people, so you can probably imagine what happened next, absolutely nothing. 'It was awful, there was no connection. The energy did not flow. Very frustrating. I then consciously decided that I'm not a typical business consultant and since then I do things my way, and it works.' She now knows that you get the clients you resonate with. The tricky thing, she says, is that you then make a choice not to conform with the group, 'that you are an exception to the organization's mainstream culture and that you don't always get the appreciation you crave.'

She has always had a love-hate relationship with wanting to belong. In her youth and student days, she regularly fell out with the group, even though she also wanted to belong. 'It was difficult because I wanted to be myself. My urge for autonomy is stronger than wanting to belong.' She once had a complete fall-out with the sorority she belonged to, was ignored for a period of time because she had dared contradict the board and an advisory committee consisting of hotshots from the business world. 'I can still see myself standing there, with people literally crossing the road and me standing alone. This is one of the moments in your life where you have to follow your heart. I knew then and still know, that I don't want to belong to just one group or bubble. I like to be in and among several groups of people.'

According to Annemarie, it is a question of having faith in life, that things will turn out all right. 'I want to keep learning, develop myself and become and be an old wise woman.' That means being and staying curious, remaining open and able to look at things differently.' Since her early thirties, her development plans have included wanting to become an old wise woman and she says, 'I am starting to get closer to it.'

Getting to Know My Own Strength

She has always been brave and inquisitive. 'I have often been alone at difficult moments in my life. Like years ago, when – within a period of six months – my business, with my business partner/best friend collapsed, as did my marriage.' She had to keep going for her two sons and for herself, 'bread needed to be put on the table.'

Two years later she slipped in a horrible way and almost lost her lower leg: 'Twenty days in hospital, six months of intensive rehabilitation and having to take my boys to school on the scoot mobile.' She was an entrepreneur, so no sickness benefits for her. Her divorce had left her with 'little financial fat on her bones.' So after six weeks she went back to her clients thanks to a student driver, first in a wheelchair and later on crutches. She did not have a partner for a long period. 'In retrospect, it was a good thing that I was alone. I had to get to know my own strength better and learn to listen to my inner voice. Of course, I had family and friends, but you really have to find the way forward by yourself.'

When it comes to being relentlessly yourself, she thinks she still has quite a bit lot to learn. 'Expressing myself, guarding my boundaries in a respectful way, holding on to things that are essentially important for the result. While remaining, of course, in contact with others and giving them space too.'

For Annemarie, being relentlessly yourself has everything to do with loving yourself. 'It is about self-acceptance. Detaching from what others think of you. To not constantly raise the bar. To deal with obstacles and conflicts and not be afraid of disconnection or temporary disruption, where you would sell yourself short.'

The life phase she is in now, is about feeling what is good for her and she is now better able to do that than ever before. 'I'm not afraid to stand up for it. In life you get put to the test a lot to become who you really are. I have had the necessary challenges.' She says she has mostly lived in the future. She held on because things would be better ahead. 'You make choices in everything that you go through. 'I always carefully weighed the interests of my family, partner and business partner against my own interests. We make choices we think are the right ones for us at that moment. I don't find looking back and having regrets, very useful.'

Looking at Myself with Gentleness

During the corona crisis Annemarie took a digital course in creative writing and drawing, in which she became very aware of how critically she had always looked at herself. 'I was given the task of looking at myself in the mirror, drawing who I saw and writing the words to go with it. I saw a mild, friendly smiling Anne looking at me. I was stunned and proud at the same time. I could not take my eyes off myself and I thought wow, you are looking at yourself with so much gentleness.' What she felt is exactly what she wants to feel when she dies, 'that I can look at myself with kindness. What I became aware of is how critical I had always been towards myself and how high I had set my bar.'

At fifty, she dares to combine the urge for autonomy, for being relentlessly herself, with kindness towards herself. 'This leads me to speak out more clearly about things that are important to me. Things that I used to brush under the carpet under the guise of the common good.' She is amazed at how strongly her children, her love, friends, and colleagues react to this gentleness towards herself and how she communicates her boundaries. 'They just take it into account which enables a dialogue about what is best for both. I also radiate somehow differently, and that resonates with others.'

She now trusts that everything will work out. 'I am exactly where I need to be. I live and enjoy much more in the present.' This brings her a lot of peace. A peace she cherishes and guards. And in that peace, she feels that there is still much more to come. 'I am far from finished here. Could I finally be becoming that old, wise woman?'

10 | **David McGowan**

The richness of being different

David McGowan (48) is publisher with roots in Ireland based in Brussels. He has been owner of Together Magazine *for years, which is a lifestyle magazine on personal development. David has been a business owner since 2006. In the past, he worked for the online business of* Elsevier Magazine. *David loves playing tennis, and although he can lose with serenity, he doesn't like losing at all.*

Reading *Rich Dad, Poor Dad* of Robert Kiyosaki was an eyeopener for him back in 2006 when he decided to start his own business. For him that was the beginning of a wonderful journey. 'When I was about seventeen or eighteen years old, I had trouble in school, I was a total rebel.' In fact, he got kicked out of four schools and ended up in a special school for dropouts.

'I couldn't stand the box that they put us in in school.' He started working at a hotel doing the dishes, working himself up to barman in his late teenage years. 'It's at the bar of that five-star hotel where I met a lot of successful people. I was inspired to go back to school and get a degree.' When he arrived back in school a friend gave him a couple of NLP-tapes, and he told David to listen to them 'These tapes were from this guy called Tony Robbins. This helped me to get my degree within one year and go to university.' After university he went and got an MBA from Boston University. 'I was beating all the odds at that stage. From a total dropout to eager to learn and develop myself.'

'Sometimes we think we have to fit into a mold, but in fact we don't.' It's the school system that forces us a bit to think like that, but we all are different. 'That is the richness of being different, that is why we need to hold on to the differences.' He thinks that that is where we can really provide value. 'If there are two minds in a room and they think alike, there is one too many.'

When he took on the magazine he wanted to communicate. 'I wanted to tell the world about this super powerful stuff that I learned so much from. That someone like me, a complete drop out, had managed to get into university and succeed.' Anyone can live the life that they want, if they want it bad enough. 'There is this powerful quote from Marianne Williamson: "Our deepest fear is that we are powerful beyond measure. It is our light, not our darkness, that most frightens us." That is exactly how it is.'

During that time, David was working in the corporate world, he found that there was little room for his creativity. And also, the fact that he had to check in and be present between certain timeframes, 'that wasn't working for me.' He was still kind of a rebel back then. He wanted to create freedom and work in his own time and design the life that he wanted to live. 'For me, freedom has always been key.'

I Was So Stripped, I Had Nothing

Through education everybody can be successful. 'Overnight success doesn't happen. It takes years and years and I have learned to never give up. Just too many people give up on their dreams and then you're "dead".' One of his dreams was to live in a mansion. 'I had a beautiful house on my dream board for years and I ended up buying it. You have to know that I have a middle-class background, so I was mortified with fear taking that step, but nevertheless, I did it.'

Sometimes people ask him if he ever wants to give up. To that he says, 'Definitely, every day I want to give up.' Even now, he has just taken over a new company, it's scary for him and it's big. 'I wonder: will I be up to the standard? There is always the self-doubt that kicks in. But then it passes and then the next day I feel lucky and blessed. I have had many challenges so far.'

When he bought the magazine back in the end of 2008 the crisis hit, by the end of 2009 he had huge debts. 'It was a tough time. As they say, the higher you go, the harder you fall.' But somehow, he knew that this was part of the journey. 'At one point I was so stripped, I had nothing. When you find out that even then, you're still fine, then it's okay.' That gave him a sense of reassurance. He continued on going, the only way was forward. 'I can't even say that I'm this relentless brave guy. I didn't have a choice. Potentially I knew I was able to make enough money to get back, but not with a normal job. As an entrepreneur we invest the money that we have, so we never have money.'

What is very interesting to see, says David, is that when you are really in trouble, something comes up. 'Like there is a turn, it's like magic, something comes to saves us if we have to be saved in that particular situation. It's the serendipity, magical, unexplainable power that comes at the right time.'

Having an Open Mind

From a reckless immature boy, I became a man, a father, a business owner. 'That was thanks to education and being open minded about it all.' For him to be himself and to stay aligned, he does his daily meditation. One of the things he does is think of three things that he is grateful for and 'I make myself really feel them. Having my own company can be scary and challenging sometimes. You can't have fear and be grateful at the same time, so this exercise helps me ground myself. Gratitude is the key to happiness, and I believe that this is the most important lesson to pass on to my kids.'

He has learned to be good to himself. One of the things he discovered in life is 'that we are all "sick" from one point of view. We all have problems with us, we get through childhood damaged and sometimes we take the rest of our lives to recover from the damages.' That rucksack could be given through generations. 'There you have a choice to cut that chain, go clean and light through life and not pass it on to your own children. By healing ourselves and being ourselves, while taking others and their feelings into account, we can fully take our role in life.'

11 | **Johanna Maria Riemen**

You can grow when you live from love

From childhood on, she has had a special gift, which she fought for years as she could not express it. It was a lonely journey, but an unavoidable one. Johanna Maria Riemen (58) is a medium and psychic and helps people, politicians and businesspeople, but also sick children, with their questions. She lives together with her partner, an artist, in Scheveningen, by the sea.

Everyone is here on Earth for the same reason, and that is to let your soul grow. She says. 'Whether you are a minister, a toilet attendant, whether you were born into society or not. We are all here to get rid of the layers of our ego that we have built up in the course of our lives. These layers are our pitfalls in thinking, our (negative) emotions, our ideas, and the patterns we have made our own and which prevent us from being ourselves. Some have more than others, which is why some have more work in soul development than others. Origins, background and education play no role here.'

She uses narcissists as an example. According to Maria, narcissists have built up many layers and have a large ego. 'Narcissism is often labelled as something psychological, but I see it differently. These are people whose soul development is still low. Others have built up less layers and are therefore further in their soul development.'

She explains that you grow your soul by increasing your self-knowledge, by gaining insight into your patterns and by clearing out what needs to go, in order to 'get to the core of your soul. If you live from a place of love, also towards others, you can grow.' You can grow for example through the people around you, your family, your partner and your colleagues at work. It doesn't really matter what kind of work you do, 'jobs are actually merely a time filler.'

A Battle with Yourself

She sees the development over the past twenty years with the advent of the computer as good, as you can contact anyone on the other side of the world within a second. Yet on the other hand, 'the downside of this shrinking of the world, is that it has also created an opportunity for evil to grow. Young people are for example confronted very early on with sex as if it were love, and I find that a great worry.' She also struggles with the hardening of people. 'We no longer walk into each other's houses as spontaneously, we hardly ever write each other a handwritten card, and everyone is always busy.'

She does see, in the face of the hardening of society, that people are increasingly becoming more conscious. 'Those who are in a higher state of consciousness are suffering from burn-out and a lot of stress. These people feel that things are not right.' They look into it, do yoga, mindfulness, meditation and seek each other out. 'Conscious becomes more conscious and that is a good thing, but it does not stop there.' She says that which can really help, 'lies within us' and yoga alone cannot solve it. It is necessary to 'clear out and broaden our consciousness and that can sometimes be a huge fight with yourself. It is certainly not easy but is the way to really take on life and discover yourself.'

Life is Tumultuous

'I don't always enjoy life here on Earth.' Maria cannot avoid 'constantly receiving information, I see what's going wrong,' which leads her to sometimes miss her open-mindedness and spontaneity. She remembers a friend telling her she was getting married. 'I knew that the relationship wouldn't last, I saw a divorce in eight years' time. At times like that, I do not like receiving information, it complicates things for me.'

She has learned to hold her mouth. She would very much like to live life in an open way but can't because of what she sees and what she receives. 'I see life as a tumultuous series of rocks, a road of trial and error, which you have to go through in order to let your soul grow. Each time you clear things out, you create space to continue. "Down here", you have to create it all yourself but "up there" it is different.'

There are many people she does not like; she is referring to the egos. 'Up there, same finds same, in the sense that you are with people at the same level of consciousness. Here it is different, people from different levels of consciousness are mixed together and that can be quite dangerous and get too close for comfort, even in your immediate circle.'

She experiences life as quite the ordeal. When she was ten or eleven, she was somewhat absent-minded, and no one knew what was wrong with her. 'I travelled *up there*' and she later wrote a book about it. 'That was an intense period. I turned against my gift. At fifteen and sixteen, I was practically a nerve patient because I could not express what I felt. No way could you talk about mediums in those days.' Hers was a lonely journey and she knew at some point she would do better to keep her mouth shut. When she was around twelve or thirteen, her parents sent her to a psychiatrist 'who said: "There's nothing wrong with her, she's just clairvoyant." I fought it, but there was no way out.' Doing other work was not an option. She worked for a while in a police office, but 'I was constantly receiving information. It just did not work for me.'

Maria often works remotely with sick children, children who do not sleep well, and people who are stressed. 'I heal remotely with photos.' She is constantly serving others.

She must distinguish 'between what I receive and what I think, because the latter is my personality and that is not what it is about, nor what people come for.' She explains that she has seven guides who provide truly clear information and directions. 'I am only a messenger. I get to see what is going on with someone, what it is really about and what is about to happen.'

She sometimes goes to a monastery or sits by the sea to keep the balance and to enjoy. 'My husband is an artist, and we have a lot in common in terms of music and culture. We go together on pilgrimages to Lourdes, to Lisieux and to Patmos.' They also go out to dinner regularly and in this way brings in lightness, which helps balances things out. In the future, what she would like most is to 'withdraw from human life' as she calls it, a bit more. To go to Normandy or Brittany with her husband and be creative, to paint more, to design things. 'Then I can let go what I am doing now a bit more.'

She has no set rituals to stay attuned. 'That doesn't work for me, it's part of me and I don't have to sit and meditate. That is the risk, that you do not do it with devotion.' She has also seen this in the monastery, nuns who do it with devotion and others who do it from a need, 'the latter does not work.'

'What I still have to learn is to ask for help for myself, because I don't really do that. I could do it, and it would also be good for me, despite the fact that it feels unnatural as I like to serve others. There is still a learning curve in that for me.'

PART 2

LETTING GO OF WHAT HOLDS YOU BACK

3

MAKING ROOM FOR ANGER AND JOY

"How we master our emotions affects the amount of pain or joy we feel." – **George Kohlrieser**

Now that you have read the thoughts and reflections around being relentlessly yourself and truly living your life, it is time to delve deeper into the topics that are linked to this and lie beneath the surface. Topics that we all have to deal with and that determine the extent to which we know, and dare to be ourselves. In this chapter I will discuss anger and joy, in the next chapter I will touch expressing sadness and acknowledging fear. I am taking you with me into Ellen's story.

Ellen recounts: *"Even as a child I was afraid of my father, he was a temperamental man. There was a lot of quarreling at home between my parents. My father worked out, was a big, strong man and had a short fuse. He ranted and raved regularly and on top of that, he hit my mother. Already as a child, I was terrified of that man. We often fled to the neighbors or to the balcony to find safety. When my parents split up, my mother, sister and I left to my grandmother's. The three of us lived in the living room of my grandmother's one-room flat, and we stood the mattresses up during the day.*

A year and a half later my mother fortunately got her own house, but soon thereafter, my parents suddenly got back together again. I found this very difficult as a child, and really didn't understand it at all. Moreover, I was angry with my mother, I couldn't understand how she could go back to my father after all the misery we had been through.

In my late thirties, my mother got cancer. On the day my mother was to get the test results and we would be told the prognosis, I was to go to the hospital with my sister and my mother. When I arrived at my parents' house, my sister was standing in the doorway making signs that they were fighting. It was once more about money and my father was beyond himself and raging at my mother in the roughest way imaginable. At that precise moment something happened in me. I felt so much anger bubbling up. I stood there, straight in front of my father as he screamed. For the first time in my life I resisted, I stood there and thought: come on then. I felt more powerful than ever before, I had reached my limit, to here and no further. My father was taken aback. I can clearly remember thinking: this is not on, mama is seriously ill. I felt I had to protect her.

My father looked at me and said: 'You are no longer my child and I do not love you anymore.' My heart was in my throat, yet I was surprisingly calm and said to my father, 'It is your inability to communicate that makes you scold mummy and no longer love me.' My father walked out. At that moment I felt a primal strength and courage, a moment later my legs started trembling and the emotions arose. I felt deeply affected and my father's remark hurt, I suffered from it for a long time. What remains when I look back, is a feeling of pride, that at that one moment I really stood up for the first time, for my mother but above all for myself."

The Four Basic Emotions

Our feelings are worth their weight in gold as they represent the voice of our souls. A silent knowing of what is good for us and what is not. Your emotions are not your feelings yet are linked to them. Our emotions create a certain feeling and feelings can lead to emotions in a positive or negative sense. You could say that we roughly have four important basic emotions, namely:
1. Anger
2. Sadness or sorrow
3. Joy
4. Fear

The language we speak in terms of emotions is a lot richer on the negative spectrum than it is on the positive one. Of the four main groups of emotions discussed in this chapter and the next, joy is the only positive one. It is interesting to note how, in the language we speak, the negative seems to prevail. What is even more important to me is the fact that that which emotions can generate, can contain something beautiful. I use the word 'can' consciously, as effort and attention are required in order to become more aware and to ensure that your insights contribute to more depth and joie de vivre.

    Emotions arise from an injured part of you. Therefore, they are not an absolute truth, but convey an important message. All it takes is for you to become aware of your emotions, take them seriously and give them space. When you do, you naturally come closer to your feelings, in fact your emotions will keep your consciousness awake. Ignoring your emotions can make you ill, it can harden you and, in the end, it will not make you happy. If the storm of emotions is intense, make sure to land, to ground in your body and sink out of your head and out of your heart. (Yes, you read correctly, also out of your heart.) It is all about finding peace within your body, when in the eye of the storm.

We are all strewn with collective themes, such as fear, emotions, and pains. No one escapes them in life, but not everyone takes them on. For some people, there is too much pain involved. When we look at each other with understanding and patience, even those who do not dare face it, we are then in loving connection with each other.

Feelings Versus Emotions

What differentiates emotions from feeling is that emotions carry a charge that nestles in your mind. Just as you are not your thoughts, nor are you your emotions, you *have* emotions. You could see your emotions, especially the loaded ones, as a wakeup call. The further you move away from your feelings, the more intense your emotional reaction will be. Emotions are caused by the sensations you feel under your skin when you are hiding or denying something. Suppressing your emotions is never a solution and is much harder to do than hiding your feelings. Feelings are usually easier to suppress, emotions search for a way out. The more you run away from your emotions, the further you get stuck and the more stress you feel. 'Emotions often have a confusing, chaotic effect; you become restless and negative, get palpitations,' as psychic, medium and author Johanna Maria Riemen says, 'it's war within.' Anger can become a powder keg if you do not learn how to control it and make room to let pressure out from time to time. More on this later.

When looking at feelings, it is important to discover where the feeling comes from. Imagine a specific feeling that you really experience and ask yourself whether this feeling comes from within, or from something outside of you. Feelings that come from the outside sometimes seem to be our own, yet they are not. Our connections with others can create the impression these feelings are ours. Taking time alone is helpful to unravel this, go for a walk or sit down somewhere quiet and ask yourself where the feeling originated and when it occurred.

"You too are a tree. During a storm of emotion come back to the trunk of the tree and not the top, which is the level of the head or the heart. Pay attention to the movement of your abdomen, and continue to breathe, then you will survive the storm of strong emotion."
– Thich Nhat Hanh

The challenge is in dosing the loaded emotions. You always have a choice between the raw emotion you feel in the moment and how you express it. With as side note that our emotional reactions can create a state of being that is not entirely controllable. You probably know the saying: 'Don't get carried away by your emotions.' But it is not that simple. Psychologist and hostage negotiator George Kohlrieser says this statement actually implies that our emotions override our thought processes. Our emotions are energy and once that energy is generated, it has to find an outlet. Once you have felt the emotion, it is often already over.

Expressing Anger Clears the Air

Not everyone expresses anger easily, yet it is sometimes necessary to create space. It stimulates you to act and create movement. I have personally experienced how you can get stuck processing a loss when you swallow your anger. My attempt to breathe away my emotions under the cloak of love did not work. It helps to let go of negative emotions and get to the core of your feelings. Anger is raw, it is the expression of your deepest desire that cannot find its way and sometimes it should be allowed to just be.

Expressing anger is about self-acceptance, allowing yourself to let it be there, and for your anger to be legitimate. Moreover, you can trust that you can express your feelings in a loving connection. Whether this be a business partnership, friendship, or relationship. As philosopher and author Pamela Kribbe says: 'It is not an aggressive energy in essence, but a deep desire to be yourself: free of old burdens. You cannot get rid of these through the heart.'

We often get angry when a situation or person is close to our heart and we feel powerless or feel that we or someone else has been wronged. Ellen's anger was an accumulation of many years of powerlessness and a feeling of injustice. Her anger had to see the light of day.

Being able to get angry is healthy and not necessarily a bad thing. When someone gets angry at you, it means they care, and are committed to you or to the situation and are taking the trouble to engage with you. The other person has to be able to provide a safe zone to receive you with your emotions. Expressing emotions is only effective, connecting and stress reducing if someone with a positive mindset can offer that safety.

The film *The Notebook*, is about real love between two people, and how love in all its vulnerability can weather storms of emotion, including anger. That safety is important to be able to let your own emotions be, and then to see and understand them. Yet many people feel inhibited to express their anger as they think it is not 'proper'. As a result, you mute the emotion in the hope that it will go away.

Earlier on I mentioned the time factor that can soften sharp edges, but just as blood needs to run its course, anger also needs to find its way to prevent it from harming you internally in the long run. Sometimes it is better to count to ten to avoid out of control behavior, which often causes more damage. We are beings of flesh and blood and sometimes find ourselves in situations, or dealing with people, where regulation does not always work. If someone for example, sees your attempt to mirror and confront as an attack, then your powerlessness and sense of justice may kick in, as in Ellen's situation at the beginning of this chapter. Getting angry is not something to be embarrassed about, it is a valuable source of information, especially if you look at how long it takes you to be yourself again and get rid of the anger.

If you seldom or never get angry, chances are you let people walk all over you. Psychologist Steven Pont says: 'People who don't get angry quickly enough, guard their boundaries so badly that they end up having almost no territory of their own.'

Expressing your anger is risky because you do not know how the other person will react, you might be rejected. Yet that should not be a reason not to, as where than anger leads is revealing. Moreover, anger does not dissolve by being suppressed and doing nothing with it.

Old Patterns

As a child, I sometimes stood on the side-line of tense situations. I was around nine years old and felt compelled to take on the role of mediator to restore peace, although I was not in a position to change the situation. I still remember that feeling of powerlessness, all I wanted was peace and harmony. Apparently, time was needed. Even though it was beyond me, I was still part of it and chose to keep quiet to not be a burden. This period of my life lasted no longer than two years, yet it felt like an eternity to me and has had a huge impact on how I deal with conflicts and fuss. That insight is crucial to me and therein lies the tension around being relentlessly myself. What I mean by this, is that striving for harmony must not come at the cost of being you and having the courage to express yourself. I increasingly have the courage to discuss things, however vulnerable I may make myself by doing so. This is all about having *trust*.

The things we experience in our early years shape us and lead us to create certain patterns. There are exceptional situations in which I can see that the resolution of issues is beyond my control, my reaction is then to run away to protect myself. Once, for example, I was invited to a professional football match. Emotions among the supporters ran high after the event. There was a lot of commotion at the exit. These kinds of situations are not a weekly occurrence in my life, and I felt the urge to run away. My sense of safety feels compromised; I can sense discomfort in my body and my reaction is 'get out of here'. Knowing where this comes from helps me, I allow myself to be there, to not judge and be gentle with myself.

We all experience situations where we are confronted with old pains or triggers of all sorts. This impacts how we approach life, how we behave in partnerships, in work relationships, in friendships and in our romantic relationship(s). Keep track of the situations in which you experience strong emotions and see if you can discover a pattern. If you find this difficult, then get help to guide you through the process, find someone to hold up the mirror so you can get to the core.

Expressing Anger as Women

When a woman gets angry or upset about something, she is rapidly dismissed as unstable, hysterical, or unpleasant. The moment you step out of line, you are scrutinized and criticized. Society punishes women's anger and praises their passivity. Women are labelled as a bitch or *iron lady* while men who show envy are perceived as powerful, strong, and decisive. There is still a lot of inequality between women and men in this respect, especially if you take a closer look at the dynamics at different life stages.

Both men and women have an important job to do when they enter their midlife phase. A phase that starts in the second half of your thirties. I will delve deeper into this elsewhere in the book, but in the context of expressing anger, it is even more poignant when you know that it is precisely women in their midlife phase who are invited to speak out and create space for their powerful male energy. That is a far cry from keeping a lid on it, muting it, and soothing it. That is being your authentic self, speaking from your heart and having the courage to own your space.

Anger is neither good or bad and is equally present in both genders. 'Ignoring your own anger would be like ignoring your own thirst,' says poet, novelist and columnist Stella Bergsma.

Letting Go of Anger

I have had an aversion to conflict and disagreement since childhood. I do not avoid them, I prefer to use the strategy of 'putting the fish on the table', as Kohlrieser calls it. That means naming the problem and exerting yourself to clear the air. I would like to share an effective ritual to express your anger and free yourself from it, in three steps. The trick with anger is learning to dose it. That means expressing what you feel and not being afraid it will not be what the other person wants to hear. It is okay to do this and allow your thoughts and feelings to exist and be seen, as long as you are respectful to the other person. It is important you recognize and acknowledge the anger, so that you can redirect the energy it releases in a positive way and come back to feelings that are pure and free of negativity.

Step 1 - Writing Out Anger

Take the person or situation you are angry with and write down everything that comes to mind in that context, and what you feel. You can use the download at www.evelienvanes.com/download. Do not write just one page, try to fill sheets with what touches you or makes you angry. If you are not so keen on the word anger, then let it go, it is about naming that undercurrent you feel. No inhibitions, no censorship, express whatever comes to mind, be as specific and detailed as possible. Keep in mind that what someone else may think of what you are committing to paper is irrelevant, it is your process and your ritual, it is to help you in your processing.

When you have got as far as you can, go and do something else, take a walk, go for a run, or sleep on it. Chances are that new points will come to mind. Dare to be yourself, be open and unashamed.

Then it is time for a farewell ritual. Find a safe place outside, use a fire bowl or anything else where you can safely burn your paper. You can also add something else to the fire if you want, maybe an object that you associate with the person or situation. Before you start burning, think about the person or the situation and express your intention to release your anger and create space for yourself. Then light the fire and let it burn!

Step 2 - Feel Gratitude

Next, in order to turn your energy around, it is advisable to reflect on what you are grateful for in the context of this situation, or person. You transform the anger into a light and positive energy of gratitude and forgiveness, of yourself and of the other(s). This also enables you to clear yourself from the burden of a potential judgment and that creates space for new experiences.

Take your time to do this exercise; you may not feel immediately up to it after the burning ritual of step 1. Be careful not to leave it too long however, or you will lose momentum. You can repeat this exercise if you feel you haven't gone deep enough. You will notice whether you have or not as you will literally feel, over the next few days, more space and the charge of the underlying emotion fading away.

Maybe you would like to save the results of this second step, for example in your *journal* if you use it for your daily or weekly thoughts. Maybe you want to write it on a loose piece of paper and then burn it, anything works.

Step 3 - Sharing Your Writing

Maybe you have a dear friend who is able to see you as you are, someone who does not judge and with whom you are 'on the same frequency'. If so, it can be liberating to share your raw writings. Be cautious and only do this with someone you trust and who can receive them from a place of love.

All the other person needs to do is listen (or read) and be present with a friendly ear. They can respond by asking further questions in order to get to the heart of the matter if necessary. It is important however that the focus remains on your process and your situation.

This is what you will gain by letting go of your anger:
1. By expressing and sharing it, you are acknowledging it is there and can no longer avoid it or push it away.
2. It helps you give it more meaning and come to deeper insights.
3. It is very liberating to move beyond any feelings of shame. It is allowing you to be relentlessly yourself.

Joy is The Spice of Life

From a ritual to get rid of anger, let us move on to joy as the spice of life. Emotions tend to alternate and feeling the one, does not mean that there is no room for the other. Joy is the second basic emotion we are addressing here. Intense joy is one of the highest frequencies of feeling there is.

When you experience true joy, you are in the highest state of being you, you feel inner peace, strength, and self-confidence. Joy is intense, deep, enriching yet often modest. In fact, we do not actually need a trigger to feel joy, it arises from a state of consciousness and comes from within. It is already in you, like a pilot light that needs little to burn bright.

It is only when you see yourself as who you really are, fully accept it and can actually be yourself, that you can derive deep joy from life. This requires an awakening, otherwise it remains a superficial pleasure, which will never touch you on a level that contributes to your life happiness.

"Many people think excitement is happiness. But when you are excited you are not peaceful. True happiness is based on peace." **– Thich Nhat Hanh**

Many people confuse joy with fun arising from a feeling of ecstasy or excitement, whereas real joy is a feeling of serenity and peace of mind. Of course, having fun and laughing is a wonderful feeling, but there are people who laugh a lot and can have fun, but do not experience joy. Joy definitely goes a layer deeper and is therefore durable, providing you with a feeling of fulfilment.

Joy for me is intensely enjoying the magic of the early morning, breathing in the fresh air. Standing after my run at the meadow's edge with the sun on my face, soaking up the rays and feeling as if I am becoming one with the sun, merging with its spirit. Astrologer, spiritual teacher, and author Barbara Hand Clow says: 'Just like plants, we humans grow from solar energy.' And that is exactly what it is. It is feeling tenderness at the sight of a swan with her young, letting your eyes dance along with a lemon butterfly flitting past. It is feeling intensely happy while searching for shells along the surf. It is the sensation of wet grass under your feet as you roam the dewy garden in your bathrobe, early morning.

Joy is also seeing the look of gratitude in your father's eyes, that you can help him in his old age. It is sitting by the fire with your loved one, a touch, a tingle on your skin, the look in each other's eyes, feeling the connection and just being with each other in silence.

Joy, above all else, is an inside feeling that all is well just as it is, without any specific reason. That is happiness. The Danish-French impressionist Camille Pissarro once said: 'Blessed are they who see beautiful things in humble places where other people see nothing.' Therein lies the secret of experiencing true joy which can be fully experienced when you are alone. Precisely because you need to be fully present and alert in the moment.

"The only way we awaken to the beautiful inner life is to first respond to the beauty outside of us. It is the vision of earthly beauty that awakens the vision of spiritual beauty." – Inayat Khan

The foundation for experiencing joy is inner peace with what is. And by 'what is', I mean being in the moment, in full awareness of what you are feeling inside. Your thoughts are not part of this, although they try to be. Your thoughts are actually an obstacle to being in the moment with what is. This is where you can experience joy in silence. It takes practice. What you can do is go outside, in the open air, and find yourself, in silence. Place your hands on your heart and *feel* what is there inside of you. Allow everything to be and remember that the space for a deep sense of joy, can only be there where deep valleys have been climbed.

Stimulating Joy

There are certainly factors that have a positive influence on your feeling of joy. They can help you pay more attention and thus activate your joy. Archbishop Desmond Tutu calls joy a 'by-product'. It is the side effect of the eight important pillars of joy that he discusses with the Dalai Lama in *The Book of Joy*. The eight pillars they mention are:

1. *Perspective*
   Being able to change your perspective, has a positive effect on your feelings. After all, you change your per-

spective based on your thoughts. Suppose you sprain your ankle while jogging and are temporarily disabled, what do you do? Do you remain captive of your pain and frustration and worry about all the things you can no longer do? Or do you choose to put things into perspective and think: it could be much worse, and I will finally get some rest. By looking at the situation you are in from a distance, you will notice that frustration gives way to acceptance and this creates room for positivity.

2. *Humility*
Wherever you are in life and whatever role you play, humility is about humanity and the art of behaving like a human being, never being superior to others. Above all, keep laughing at your own imperfections, it will stimulate your sense of joy.

3. *Humor*
Laughter leads to relaxation and contributes to feeling good. Not always taking yourself so seriously, for example. Another case is funerals, how striking is it that funerals are usually followed by an occasion for laughter? The tension falls away as people connect and there is room for humor, this fuels joy.

4. *Acceptance*
Acceptance is about taking life for what it is. It allows you to relax and stop resisting what is, and to stop desiring the things that are behind you.

5. *Forgiveness*
Forgiveness is about taking charge of your own life and of your feelings. Forgiveness is healing and enables you to let go of the past. Otherwise, you will be left with bitterness and anger. Forgiving those closest to us is usually the hardest as it affects us the most.

6. *Gratitude*
   There where acceptance is not turning your back on reality, gratitude is embracing this reality. Gratitude is to count your blessings and leads to optimism and positive feelings.
7. *Compassion*
   We are social beings. Compassion is helping others carry their pain, this increases our feeling of joy. We are then connected to the other person and for a moment forget our own worries. To show compassion for another, it is important to be compassionate towards yourself. When for example, you see an elderly woman with a walker drop a bar of chocolate in the supermarket. The very act of helping her pick up the bar makes you feel euphoric.
8. *Generosity*
   Generosity is on the same line as compassion and is not only about material things, but also about generosity in giving time, attention, sharing knowledge and wisdom and offering security. Organizations that focus on and care for people tend to be more successful. The Dalai Lama also calls generosity 'wise selfish'. Taking care of others and helping them is the way to make yourself happier and discover your own joy.

Some of the pillars we have just touched, such as humility, acceptance, forgiveness, and gratitude, will be discussed in more detail in separate chapters.

You may be thinking that your life is too hectic for you to have rest and be able to experience these moments of joy, but where there is a will, there is a way. It does however require you make time for it and find the inner peace to allow it to enfold. The energy that deep joy sparks is a catalyst for more and will also bear fruit in your work. You could call joy 'contagious', both in terms of your own energy and its influence on others. How wonderful to be surrounded by joyful people. You can influence this, and you can start today.

> **Moments of Joy**
>
> This is a good moment to reflect on joy in your life. Answer the following two questions based on your situation:
> 1. When do you experience the sensation of real joy in your life? Describe these moments in all details, without forgetting colors and smells, as if it were happening in the here and now. Just as I described above with very concrete situations. Feel the difference between moments of fun and moments of deep joy.
> 2. Looking at the eight pillars of joy described above, what can you already do differently in your life today to feel more joy? Go through all the pillars and reflect on what you want to pay more attention to and how you want to go about this.

- ∞ Feelings are usually easier to suppress; emotions seek a way out.
- ∞ Emotions come from a wounded part of yourself, they are not an absolute truth but carry an important message.
- ∞ Being able to recognize and acknowledge anger is important so you can redirect the released energy in a positive way and regain pure feelings, free of negativity.
- ∞ Real joy is about a sense of inner peace.
- ∞ A feeling of joy is contagious; both in terms of your own energy and in terms of the influence on others.

4

EXPRESSING SADNESS AND ACKNOWLEDGING FEAR

"You can cry, you can feel miserable. Don't try to deny the suffering or you will deceive yourself. Give it time, surrender to the suffering and tell yourself this is part of life." – **Paulo Coelho**

Sadness exists for a reason; it has a function. It draws attention so you can get to the source of the sadness and free yourself from it, enabling you to open your heart once more. In this chapter, I will be discussing the basic emotions of sadness and fear and the importance of expressing your grief. This includes giving yourself permission to be completely yourself. We will also look at rejection as a trigger for grief and tips for dealing with it. Furthermore, we will be looking at fear and I will help you uncover your greatest fear and realize what knowing this brings you.

In recent years I have met several people, mostly men, who had no clue what to do with their grief. Like Steven.

Steven is a fifty-two-year-old man who shared at table with me that the last time he had shed a tear, was at his mother's funeral, already ten years ago. It certainly wasn't because his life had gone smoothly in recent years; he had been through a lot since. He had had a long and debilitating business conflict that had caused him a lot of stress and sleepless nights.

He also noticed that he was not managing to be himself at home and this frustrated him enormously. He was not managing to improve the situation with his wife, he felt lonely, even though he was longing for love and warmth and so was his wife. The home situation was stuck in a rut. On top of that, Steven's relationship with his brother had been difficult for years. They hardly spoke to each other and it was eating away at him.

So, what did he do? He fled into hard work, focused on running a business, looked for as many distractions as possible and ran from his pain and sorrow. He sat opposite me like a lost man, utterly exhausted, and he looked it. He came to me wondering why his company had stopped doing well whereas he was working his tail off.

Steven's story is no exception and shows how much impact silencing your emotions can have on your life, your business wellbeing and success, on everything. It is a pattern that takes some doing to break. We started working together, I helped him get closer to himself, to see himself as he was. By learning to distinguish between head (thoughts) and heart and to go back to his own identity, including his core values, deepest desires and to detach from what has shaped him. I helped him get back to his own roots in order to feel how far he had strayed from his true self. How his thoughts had determined his self-image and how he had taken that on as being 'true'.

He had a breakthrough and discovered that he held the key to change and when to apply the brakes when he risked drifting away from his authentic self. It didn't take long before he gave himself permission to be who he really was and also to make room for his sadness. At home, this led him to open a dialogue with his wife where they could talk to each other in all vulnerability.

Bottling up grief seems an easy solution, yet it leads to it being magnified on the inside. It can make you ill, as in Steven's example, whereby his appearance unmistakably told the story of his inner world. Water should flow; stagnant water is rotten water. It is the same with tears. Letting tears flow cleanses our eyes and relieves the heaviness we feel when we try to push our sorrow away. Pain and sorrow are part of life and it is by experiencing that pain that we can appreciate the beautiful things in life.

"It's okay to cry when there's too much on your mind. The clouds rain too when things get heavy." – Prince Ea

Crying is our natural way of expressing emotions and an essential part of the process of expressing and processing any form of grief. In his book *Hostage at the Table*, Kohlrieser states that one of the reasons why men die an average of seven to twelve years before women, may be linked to their finding it harder to cry and express their grief.

You are not acknowledging your feelings when you cannot express your tears of sadness. Do you hold your tears back when you are watching a film with someone else? How beautiful and wonderful to let our tears flow and let go of what the other may think. That is being relentlessly yourself. Should the other person comment on it, then it says more about their own discomfort than about you. Furthermore, sharing grief with someone can contribute to a feeling of deep connection with yourself and with the other. You are then in such pure alignment with your authentic self, that you give expression to your grief from your very 'being'. You are touched by the reflection of something deep within. By sharing this, you touch others at a deeper level, which enables you to potentially connect with each other from there.

It is healing to share your sorrow with others, by talking about it and letting your tears flow in the presence of another. It contributes to a healthy processing of your inner pain. Sorrow will find its way out at some point. Provide space for that which needs to be released and discover how much relief and relaxation it brings.

There is often beauty to be found in the source of your sadness. Poet, philosopher, and artist Khalil Gibran says: 'When you are sorrowful look again in your heart, and you shall see that in truth you are weeping for that which has been your delight.'

The Impact of Rejection

Everyone encounters rejection in their life. Rejection can lead to great sadness. It starts early in life, at school for example when team members are chosen in the gym class, or later on, when you fail an exam, are rejected for a job, or when a friend no longer wants to hang out with you. Rejections affect us, elicit emotional pain, and can lead to grief. It can affect your mood and have impact on your self-confidence. There are also people who recur to anger and rage when faced with rejection, while others withdraw quietly.

The greatest damage from rejection, is self-inflicted. Our natural response is not to lick our own wounds, but to become self-critical. Most people almost automatically assume that a rejection is a personal rejection. This reaction is, in most cases, unjustified. The rejection is often caused by circumstances, timing, different needs or simply the fact that there is no fit. We react by immediately poring over our imperfections. After all, you want to understand why you were rejected. Psychologist Guy Winch gives three specific tips on how to deal with rejection:

1. Have zero tolerance for self-criticism. Reflecting on what happened is understandable, but be careful not to hurt yourself unnecessarily with self-criticism.
2. Revive your self-worth. It is effective to focus on your qualities and your value instead of listing your shortcomings.
3. Be more sociable. Connecting with others makes you feel loved and valued and contributes to your self-esteem. You are able to shift your attention for a moment.

Beyond the Paralysis of Fear

Rejection can not only lead to sadness, but it can also cause intense tension and fear. Fear is the fourth basic emotion discussed here. I shall share Renée's story in this context.

"Something happened last week in my practice," says Renée, who works as a therapist. *"It reminded me of a moment when I was about ten years old. I was at primary school and we*

were skating with school on natural ice. It was a race on a big pond in the woods. I noticed, after several laps, that I was skating in the lead. I could no longer hear anyone around me, no one overtook, and I was way ahead of the rest. I remember, as if it were yesterday thinking something was wrong, I must have done something wrong, this can't be right, I must stop. And I did. I can still clearly recall how I felt. I stood still, more or less glued to the ice, legs trembling, wondering what was going on. My thoughts were all over the place, but what prevailed was a feeling of doubt and disbelief. After waiting a while, the others skated around the bend and I was able to join the rest. In the end, I crossed the finish line in second or third place. I was ashamed that I had not continued, that I had stopped and let the others pass in front.

I was bullied a lot at school, I made myself small, despite being tall and quite strong at a young age. That process of making myself small started at home. Last week, in my practice, something happened during a conversation with a client, an intelligent, friendly, and somewhat domineering man in his mid-forties, an entrepreneur with two businesses. He overwhelmed me when he came in, with a number of questions prior to our session. He asked: 'Can anyone learn to do what you do?' His question made me feel insecure and without thinking much, I answered: 'Yes, anyone can.' At that moment I felt just like that ten-year-old girl skating on the pond." A tear rolls down Renée's cheek as she tells the story, and she continues. "Self-doubt set in and I did exactly the same, kept myself small, denied myself. Why should I be able to do something that someone else can't? I felt sad and deeply affected after the conversation, with the same feeling as back then: it can't be that there is something I can do better than the rest."

Renée's story depicts how you can sometimes find yourself in situations, where you are thrown back on a past event in which fear has taken root. It is the inner child she carries with her as an adult woman, who wants to be seen and longs to be recognized. A recognition that only she can give herself.

Renée continues: *"I had a breakthrough recently during a retreat I attended on returning to your inner child. For years I have felt that there is still something in me, that goes back in my family history, and hinders me in my work and life in general. From the moment I entered the training room I felt a lump in my throat, a combination of anger and fear. I noticed how oppressive and intimidating I found the anger expressed by the men within the group. When it was my turn, a real tidal wave of anger erupted. I went back in time and remembered as a child that my grandfather gave us girls a guilder for our birthdays and the boys a rijksdaalder (a two-and-a-half-guilder piece). I can still picture him saying: 'Here you go, at least you have something too.' Just thinking back, I could feel the anger and incomprehension rising within me.*

I also remembered his tradition of opening a bank account for boys born into the family, as a present, whereas my sisters and I did not get one. My grandfather was belittling towards girls and women in the family. I did not know any better.

During the retreat, I started feeling that he had never wanted to see me for who I really am. I realized that this was where my 'feeling inferior to others', especially men, originated, in the connection with my grandfather. Now that I know this, it frees up space for me to accept that I have this trigger, but that it has nothing to do with reality."

Emotions are there to be expressed, often we want to understand them. The understanding around what was going on usually transpires after a while. Renée's example shows how valuable it is to recognize the origin of the emotions and to understand how they have taken hold of your system. This helps you to accept what is, better and faster. It is okay that it affects you, time and time again, but it is once you no longer lose yourself in it, that healing takes place.

Fear or Trust and Love

Fear and courage are not far apart. Action is what is needed to bridge the gap between the two. Many people live from a place of fear. They are afraid of not doing well in life, afraid to take the leap, to have a difficult conversation, to stand up for themselves or they are afraid of death. Plenty of reasons to see problems everywhere. Much of the fear people have is unrealistic fear, fear that our thoughts perceive as true. These thoughts haunt us and drive us crazy.

Fear does not come from the heart. It is linked to the mind and all it does is paralyze. In talking to clients, I often see people driving themselves mad, stuck in a maze, with signposts for fear at every corner.

Everyone has fears and we all have to deal with them to a greater or lesser degree. Sometimes we are afraid of the power we feel within us, we may not know what to do with it. A feeling felt more by women than men, is the fear their inner power is greater than they think they can handle. Many women fall into the habit of viewing their potential through the eyes of inferiority. Women in particular, tend to work below their 'capabilities', in jobs that allow them to combine their working life with a family. You still see this a lot in the Netherlands, but also in many other developed countries. In Scandinavia, women work more, and longer hours and the childcare system is designed accordingly. Besides the practical matters that influence this, it is often linked to fear and not claiming your space, resulting in a consistent gnawing feeling within.

"The most fearful people can become the most courageous." – **George Kohlrieser**

Take a moment to investigate which fears are part of behavioral patterns you have internalized. Now, each time you encounter a situation around fear you can ask yourself:
- Is this a real fear and where does it come from?
- What would happen if I now choose trust and love?

Let us take an example. You are working on a large project and after an important project meeting, you have a chat with the program director. He says, 'Thank you for your thorough preparation and I am pleased that good progress has been made.'

You talk some more and then a specific situation comes up during the meeting and he says: 'What I did want to tell you is that I didn't find your remark about the approval process during the meeting very appropriate.' At that point, you have a choice: do you go on the defensive or do you take a deep breath, ask further clarification and then thank him for his feedback? Are you able to do so? When you are, you are choosing trust and love over fear. People who think in terms of possibilities and choose love and trust over fear, take responsibility for their own lives through introspection and deepening.

Knowing what your greatest fear in life is, is worthwhile in order to get to know yourself even better. For in your greatest fear lies your grip on life. When asked what your greatest fear is, Kohlrieser would say: 'Put the fish on the table with yourself,' meaning what is it really all about? I personally pondered some time myself on how to get to the core of this question. I did it by taking time to feel and by questioning myself further and further to get a layer deeper. Sparring with someone else helps you see whether you have got to the core of the matter. You will know when you have got to the root of your fear. My greatest fear for example is that I lose my ability to fall back on my primal trust. My primal trust is also my life line, my foundation in life. As long as I remain connected to it, I feel that I am alive.

> **Greatest Fear**
> What is your greatest fear in this life?
> Think about it for a while and find someone with whom you can share your greatest fear. Sharing will help you see if you got to the heart of the matter. Get someone to keep on questioning you.

Fear of Death

The world we live in is geared towards prolonging lives, but sometimes the soul is ready for its journey of discovery in this life. Fearing death can be quite weary. How do you look at death? Does it unsettle you, do you give it any thought, or does it leave you indifferent?

If you recognize a fear of death, it might make to ask yourself what exactly it is that frightens you. Is it losing the people you love, or the fear of leaving them behind without you, or do you feel resistance because you are not yet 'finished' in this life?

"When you do not dive deep into life's secrets, have no knowledge of life and death, then you become the slave of disappointment, and that disappointment is death. It is man's fault that he wants to let the mortal part of his being live on; that brings disappointment. For only he knows the mortal part of his being and identifies with it." **– Inayat Khan**

What I like about Khan's statement is that many people identify with the material, being your body and life on Earth. While your soul is infinite and never dies. Fear of death doesn't actually do you any good; it's a negative emotion that only holds you back from enjoying life as it is. Fear of death, moreover, prevents you from living life to the full. Psychiatrist Elisabeth Kübler-Ross says: 'You cannot live until you are willing to die.' A cramped hold on life is an obstacle to living it. Death for me, is leaving the material behind so that your soul can pursue its journey of development. Each human being is so much more than a physical reality. From the perspective of our soul, life is just a page in an endless story. I grant it to everyone to feel trust and not fear the transience of this earthly life.

For me, increasing self-awareness and staying true to myself contribute to surrendering to life. That means that when death is near, and I feel that this is the intention, I accept it. Which, by the way, does not mean I have no zest for life, on the contrary, in fact it is greater than ever. My journey of discovery is not yet over, I still have much to learn and to bring to others.

Urge to Control

"It's our holding on to, our need for control, that keeps us from exactly what we desire." - **Barbara Hand Clow**

Whether you like it or not, you have no control over life. This urge to control comes from fear and the strain to avoid pain. You think you can suppress your fear by controlling a situation but often achieve the opposite. Your fear is only amplified and fed. In this way you are also holding yourself away from your desires. 'You can never really get a grip on life through thinking. Thinking is powerless when it comes to the real questions of life,' says Kribbe.

I regularly see clients in my practice who struggle with their tendency to control. These are often patterns from our upbringing, such as judgments, opinions and doubts passed on by parents and guardians. This may seem part of you but is often adopted behavior that is not inherent in our nature. Differentiating the two is not always easy. What is part of your nature and what is nurture; that which has shaped you along the way? I will take you into Laura's story.

Laura has a job for three days a week working for an employer and is also an entrepreneur. Her dream is to run her business full time and be able to quit her job. Her fear of taking that step holds her back as her job gives her a sense of finan-

cial security, and she is not ready yet to let go of that. She has been struggling with this choice for years, even though deep down she feels that this is what she wants.

Laura's mother now has dementia and lives in a nursing home. She visits her mother once in a while but can't really make much contact with her anymore. Laura explains about her mother's urge to control. How as a child she used to obey her mother, so she did not cause any stress and panic to her mother. When her mother for example told her to wear a helmet on her bike to school, she did so even though she was the only one wearing a helmet. Later, when she wanted to go to the cinema with friends, she was not allowed to cycle at dusk. She had to be brought and picked up.

Laura is now forty and has noticed that she has the same tendency to curb her fear by exercising control. She does this with her four-year-old daughter, although in her own way and less compulsively, she feels. The fact is that it disturbs her that her mother's fear lives on in her. She recognized the pattern since becoming a mother. She finds it stressful and it also has an impact on her work and the choice she has been circling for years. She is afraid to leave her job even though the job drains her of energy and brings her no satisfaction.

Motherhood has accelerated Laura's awareness of the stressful pattern of exercising control. Something that is not part of her nature. These patterns are often part of people's lives for a long time. Breaking free from these patterns starts with recognizing and acknowledging that something is not actually yours.

One way of distinguishing nature from nurture, is to go back to your early years as a child. What was going on inside of you, how did you approach life, how brave were you and what was your character? Clarifying this often helps answer the question of whether something is inherently yours or not. Then the question is: if it is not yours, then whose is it and are you prepared to part with it and give it back? It sounds simple enough. Putting it into practice is harder, but making the decision is an important first step. Next, you can use a ritual to let go, or leave behind what is not yours. You can choose for example to bury something that you associate with the acquired pattern. You can do this in your own garden or in the woods. Even though the trigger will most likely remain, the ritual helps you to let go and to remind yourself that this is no longer yours. This makes it easier to put it aside.

Showing Up in The Arena

Most people dislike making mistakes. There is however no real growth without sticking your neck out, taking risks and 'showing up in the arena', as professor and author Brené Brown says. Being in the arena inherently means balancing on the edge and daring to make mistakes. It is the setbacks in your life which teach you the most.

Standing in the arena also requires you to show vulnerability. Vulnerability is having the courage to stand in the arena without having at that moment control over the outcome or result. The degree of vulnerability you dare show reflects your courage. There is, moreover, no creativity without vulnerability. You can only discover your unique gift and use it in your life and work, when you dare to be vulnerable. Imagine that you are an artist, that you spend months working on a painting in which you have put your very heart and soul. Can you imagine how vulnerable this feels? How much courage does it take to bring this work of art into the world?

For me, showing up in the arena means going off the beaten track and letting yourself be led by what feels good because you are letting the 'voice of your soul speak', as Kribbe calls it. This may lead to irritation in some areas of your life, in your work, in friendships and relationships. That chafing will remain until you decide to remain true to yourself.

When you are able to free yourself from the thoughts of 'what will others think?' You take a crucial step towards being relentlessly yourself and owning your place in life from your unique gift. That is what it is all about. Stay focused and if you find it difficult, name what it is you need in order to let go of what other people find and think. What others think and feel is irrelevant. All the people you know, who you admire for being successful, have made mistakes and faced challenges time and time again.

> **Exercising Control**
> Answer the following questions in the context of exercising control. You can use the download at www.evelienvanes.com/download.
> 1. What are the things you like to be in control of?
> 2. And why is that? Be as specific as possible about what drives you to exercise control.
> 3. What do you need to be able to let go of what others think of you?

Fear is always a lack of self-confidence. Author Jed McKenna (pseudonym) says: 'All fear is ultimately fear of no-self.' It takes courage to eradicate fear. Once you are ready to step into that arena, make sure you are surrounded by people who love you for who you are. People who encourage you and dare to be honest with you. People who love you for who you are, not in spite of your faults, but because of the diamond in the rough that you are.

- ∞ Sadness has a function. Get to the source of your sadness to free yourself from it and open your heart.
- ∞ Rejection can lead to great sorrow and we all have to deal with it.
- ∞ Fear does not come from the heart. It is linked to our mind and it paralyses you.
- ∞ Your greatest fear is at the same time your life line, your foundation in life.
- ∞ Fear is always a lack of self-confidence. It takes courage to eliminate fear.
- ∞ The urge to control comes from fear and cramping on to avoid pain. Work on your self-confidence and take a step in the right direction to overcome fear.

5

LETTING GO OF EXPECTATIONS

Having expectations can have a strong influence on how we stand in life and how we feel. Being relentlessly yourself means walking your own path, a path where you are in constant connection with others. We have expectations of others and others of us, both at work and at home. In this chapter, I will be discussing both perspectives and what it takes to let go of the expectations that may be a burden to both yourself as well as others. Besides that, there is also something beautiful in expectations, as therein lies a desire.

The expectations you have of others can lead you to feel cornered. This happens at work through the goals you set, but also in collaborative relationships and privately in friendships and relationships. Expectations in the realm of relationships are the hardest to let go. Having expectations puts us in the position of being potentially disappointed. When we have no expectations, everything that turns up is a surprise. It is not so much the situations or people that disappoint us, it is our high expectations. Elisa and Paul's expectations led to a deception.

Elisa and Paul were travelling together through South America. A beautiful journey through Patagonia they had been looking forward to for a long time. Elisa enjoyed it from day one, whereas Paul was taking longer to relax and find his feet. Elisa speaks of how 'dark' his moods were at times, in particular the first days. After a week nevertheless, they found each other again and all together it was a wonderful holiday. The evening before they were to fly home, he surprised her with a marriage proposal. She had not seen this coming, but was pleasantly surprised. There was no official ring yet, but Paul had brought a mock one that he slipped on her finger.

Once back they had occasional conversations about the engagement ring and what kind of ring it should be. Elisa shared her fervent wish for a vintage ring as a symbol of their love. A ring with character, a piece of jewelry with a story, that would fit her personality.

When Paul found the perfect ring, the excitement was great. She told how Paul had excitedly slipped the box under her nose during a romantic dinner. She never forgot the moment she opened the box. She saw a classic ring with a whopper of a diamond glittering at her. He looked at her with pride: 'Isn't it beautiful?'

She felt the blood drain from her face and had to pull herself together to avoid collapsing. The disappointment on her face was hard to hide. She kissed him and thanked him for the beautiful ring, but felt both sad and guilty at the same time. Guilty because she felt she should not be disappointed by such a huge 'rock'. She was wondering what the conversations over the past few months had meant. Elisa was very confused and uncomfortable with the situation.

This story is about expectations, good intentions, and how

painful their effect can sometimes be. About the danger of staying in your own cocoon and failing to connect with each other. How he chose a ring with the best of intentions but bypassed who she was. And how she struggled with her expectations and guilt because she did not want to appear ungrateful, yet felt sad that he had not really seen and heard her. You might not be surprised to hear that this wedding did not materialize. The challenge in every connection is to be true to yourself and really see the other for who they are.

Letting Go of a Set Format

Things always work out in life, but not always in the way we expected them to. To live completely free of expectations, is a noble goal to have, but do not let it become a goal in itself. Expectations, moreover, make you aware of what you want to create in life. Behind the expectation lies a desire which comes from your heart.

What you want to avoid is getting stuck in the precise form in which a certain desire presents itself and when it should occur. These thoughts then become expectations. When you let go of a specific format, you give yourself the space to look at what is presenting itself with an open mind and heart. It could just be that your desire becomes reality without you even noticing it simply because you do not recognize it as such.

An example: suppose you have registered and paid for a training course, and you go there with high expectations. You want to get inspired, meet three potential clients and see a return on investment within three months. How different would it be, were you to approach the training with the desire for interesting encounters, sincere connections, and inspiration? How much more space would this give you, removing the pressure, allowing yourself to experience a nice day and open up to everything that arises?

Hence, goal setting is also about expectations. Many people set goals, thinking it brings focus and helps to progress. It's nice to know what you want, but with goal setting too we run the danger of creating so much pressure that it starts working against you. The result being that you then attract scarcity as you are fixated on what is not yet there. One-sided focus on goals creates expectations and can lead to frustration.

When you live and work based on intentions, expressed in love and inspiration, you focus your attention on the feeling you want to bring about. You then let it go and lay the most fertile ground for beautiful things to come into being.

> **Your Expectations**
>
> What expectations do you have, and how does this affect the open-mindedness with which you approach your work and your life? Ask yourself the following questions:
> 1. Define which expectations you want to map out. Around for example: your company, a cooperation partner, your client, your manager, your colleague, the team in which you work, your relationship, a friend.
> 2. What are your expectations? Be as detailed as possible, be honest with yourself and write down everything that comes to mind.
> 3. Which expectations do you want to let go of?

4. What do you need in order to let go of these expectations?
5. Do you want to take it one step further? If so, discuss your intentions with someone you trust. Sharing helps you to sharpen your focus on what you might be able to let go of.

Parental Expectations

You have just mapped out your own expectations. You also have to deal with the expectations of others, for example those your parents have of you. This can be a red thread through your life. It can be asphyxiating when these expectations do not match the image you have of your life. We all grow up in a family, with parents or guardians who have expectations of us. These are sometimes explicitly expressed, but are usually subtle and therefore no less prominently present in your system.

Detaching from your parent's expectations can be a relief, but in practice often goes hand in hand with pain and sorrow. Children's loyalty to their parents is usually so great that these relationships, also known as *vertical relationships*, can take a blow. This is different with *horizontal relationships*, such as with a partner, a friend, or a cooperation partner. The difference lies in the fact that love here is not usually as unconditional as the one that naturally exists between children and their parents and vice versa.

I myself was in a relationship with a man who swore that he loved me unconditionally. I once asked him how he saw it. My question irritated him; he thought his words were enough. Then he would say: 'It is there, what more do you want?' My experience in horizontal relationships is that love can be intense and beautiful when actions, words and feelings reinforce each other. The most important thing is to be yourself, to really see others as who they are and never take anyone for granted. This has nothing to do with unconditional love.

I come from a family in which both parents studied. My father received his doctorate a few years before my brother and later I were born. The expectation to study was clear. I am of the generation where 'a smart girl is prepared for her future' and I conformed to this expectation. I did two studies more or less by the book, passed my driving test in one go, following tradition, and climbed the career ladder after my studies. I knew no better and was encouraged to do so. I am grateful to my parents for the encouragement and opportunities they gave me. It opened doors for me.

Before, I never consciously experienced my parent's expectations as a 'burden'. It was only when I got older and came closer to my full identity that I felt I was different and wanted to make other choices. That I wanted to give more room to my creative side, that I wanted to take risks and discover what I wanted and why. Plotting your own path in life is your own responsibility and it took time for me.

> **Parent or Guardian Expectations**
> What expectations did your parents or guardians have of you? It does not matter whether your parents are still alive or not. The expectations of our parents and guardians remain a part of our life, as they become anchored in our system.

Maybe you have children of your own and recognize having expectations from the perspective of a parent. There are many parents for example, who would like their children to achieve what they themselves have not. That can create a lot of pressure. Whether we do it consciously or not (mostly not), all parents give their children messages. The parent's frame of reference is the starting point, and the character of the children, and their possibilities and limitations, are often ignored.

Then there are parents who allow their own life happiness to depend on the well-being and/or performance of their children. This creates a great impact and often only reveals itself later on in life, when you become more self-aware and break free from the patterns that have shaped your upbringing. Children are usually very loyal to their parents, regardless of their age. They want to satisfy their parents' demands and tend to bend over backwards out of love for them and to be assured of their love. The risk however is that they ignore their own desires and give and sacrifice a lot for their parents. This can create an unhealthy dynamic of expectations and loyalty, robbing yourself of the chance to take your own path and do things your own way.

I am a mother myself and believe a solid education is a good foundation to have but is not everything. Whichever choice you make, your study period is above all a phase of self-discovery and finding your way towards maturity. It doesn't really matter what kind of study you do, as long as you do something that makes you feel good and that creates movement.

I see it in my daughter, who had to choose her subject cluster for school. She was guided in her choice by her passion for sports and health, which she has had since childhood. I am her biggest fan, encouraging her to follow her heart. It is better to do your best for subjects you like than to work for something you feel little for.

Every single human being is free to learn their own lessons and find their way in life. We cannot protect each other from bumps and setbacks, nor is that the intention. There is no such thing as a flawless upbringing and education, and one could wonder if that would be desirable anyway. What could be more valuable than to give your children luggage and experiences so that they can go out into the world on their own two feet? Not everything goes smoothly in life. Falling down and getting up again are part of it. That is what life is. By learning to believe in yourself and discover who you really are, you can free yourself from the expectations of others. In this way, you can start living your own life.

- ∞ To live completely free of expectations is a noble goal, but do not make it a goal in itself.
- ∞ The beauty of having expectations is that they also withhold a desire from the heart.
- ∞ One-sided focus on goals creates expectations and can lead to frustration.
- ∞ With intentions, you focus your attention on the feeling you want to bring about. This is the most fertile ground for beautiful things to arise.
- ∞ By learning to believe in yourself and discover who you really are, you free yourself from the expectations of others.

6

ACCEPTING WHAT IS

Letting go is not always easy, but sometimes holding on to something or someone is even more difficult and painful. For me, relationships, including family and love relationships, are important learning opportunities to get to know myself even better. To stay close to my core and discover what that 'self' really is. And to allow myself to be relentlessly myself, in all respect for others of course. Accepting and letting go are indispensable topics in this process and every human being has to deal with them. In this chapter, I will discuss both subjects and you will discover that accepting precedes being able to really let go.

Many of us experience loss in one form or another. There are sometimes situations where closure is unfortunately impossible, because someone is far away or is no longer here. However difficult this may be, there is no point in resisting. This requires accepting what is, here and now, and working on yourself to heal your pain and sorrow. Doing so in such a way that you can move on and do not take your pain into the world of others who have nothing to do with it. I once read a quote from an unknown source: 'If you don't heal what hurt you, you'll bleed on people who didn't cut you.'

Letting go without being able to get closure with someone, is learning to limit the seemingly bottomless pit of grief that you experience. You, basically, are the one who can give yourself everything you need. You might wish for something or someone to save you or ease your pain, but that is precisely not the intention. If there is disharmony in your life, it is there for a reason. Sometimes people disappear from our lives and situations change. This creates room for new people and new experiences. You can rely on that. Some people are with you for a season, some for a reason and others for a lifetime. That reason can be, for example, that you have something to learn from that person.

To take on life means going into that pit with an open heart and open eyes. It means allowing the despair and misery to be, until you sense there is space again and can feel your own heartbeat and breath again. Everything flows within, your cells renew over and over, and you are constantly in motion. It is only when you are reconnected with your soul that can you feel inner peace and freedom. Reconnecting with your inner child and feeling what it needs, can be helpful. In chapter nine, I will be sharing an exercise to get in touch with your inner child.

Running away is not an option, especially not by rehashing questions about the other, as you will not get an answer anyway. Whatever happens, it is always about your part in this, about what you can change, and that is yourself. Remember in everything that happens in your life: 'This too shall pass.' Everything is temporary, that goes for the low points but also for the beautiful things in your life and work.

If you can be grateful for everything in your life, every experience, every tear, every scar on your skin and wound in your heart, then you are walking the path in this life envisaged by your soul. We never stop learning, so is the dynamic of life. There will be new challenges that will bring you anew depth and joy. Welcome to life as it is meant to be.

"Your moments of deepest despair are in fact also the times when you are at your most honest, most lucid. That is precisely when you look without blinders, and see things as they are." – Jed McKenna

Experiences of intense pain and grief can form a turning point in your development, at least if you choose to face them. This means surrendering to what is and living through the unease, the emptiness, and the pain. In such a way that, from there, you discover or recover inner peace and strength, at your own pace. It takes time. In fact, 'emptiness is an illusion', as Christina von Dreien says. In reality, 'emptiness' does not exist at all. It is merely your perception, because emptiness is also energy.

Let it be clear that no one in life is spared learning to accept and let go. We all experience it differently. What one person may live as a catastrophe from a business point of view, another may experience as a struggle or merely a challenge. Someone once said to me: 'How sad that you have been so damaged in your relationships.' This is touching and is said with the best of intentions, but it ignores the other person's process. I needed those lessons to learn about myself and life. Let me share in this context the story of a woman who wanted to free a butterfly.

A woman found a cocoon enclosing a butterfly, the cocoon had only a small opening. She looked at the cocoon and saw a butterfly struggling for hours to manoeuvre itself through the small opening. Until suddenly nothing happened, all was still, it seemed as if the butterfly was stuck. The woman could not bear it and decided to help the butterfly. She took a pair of scissors and cut the cocoon to give the butterfly some space. The butterfly now emerged, it had a swollen body and small shriveled wings. The woman watched and waited for the butterfly to spread her wings. That did not happen.

The butterfly spent the rest of its life unable to fly. She could crawl with her tiny wings and swollen body. Despite the woman's loving heart and good intentions, she had not understood that the cocoon's small opening served a function. The struggle that the butterfly had to go through herself, was to send the moisture from her body towards her wings so she could fly the moment she emerged from the cocoon.

The moral of this story is that our struggles in life are there to develop and (re)discover our inner strength. *That* is the evolution of our consciousness.

"Life provides you with the experiences that help you most in the evolution of your consciousness."
– Eckhart Tolle

To Process is a Verb

Acceptance is a conscious choice to take matters into your own hands. It is then a process by which you learn, little by little, to put up less resistance to what you are going through. You can only release, once you stop resisting. Letting go of disturbing thoughts comes easier to some than to others. The process of acceptance is a life lesson that simply takes time and attention. Time alone can ease the pain, but it does not automatically take it away. To process is not a verb for nothing, it requires consciously creating movement.

We can understand with our minds how important it is to accept and let go, but what makes this such an ordeal for many of us? Each person is different and is at a different phase of self-knowledge and development. Each person furthermore is wired differently and therefore has his or her own pace of acceptance and release. Nevertheless, one thing is true and that is, in matters touching on things and people with whom we are connected from the heart and soul, it takes time to heal. This simply cannot be rushed if you want to come to terms with yourself on a deeper level.

If you hide your head in the sand or flee, the boomerang will sooner or later come back to you. You cannot escape the important lessons that you have to learn in life. The issue may return under a different guise, but the impact will be similar and possibly even greater.

You only feel the benefits of letting go once it is done. So often we know and feel deep inside that something is not right. If only we were more faithful to that feeling.

"The pain you are experiencing now is like a stone falling into water and causing many ripples on the surface. The effect of a painful or traumatic experience ripples over time, and you will sense these ripples at other times and places and come to understand and value

that experience. The understanding that you develop later will return like a balm to the past and heal old wounds." – **Pamela Kribbe**

It sometimes seems difficult in the moment itself to understand why something is happening, what the intention or message behind it is. Everything that happens in our lives takes on meaning over time. I learned a long time ago the principle of the 'circle of influence', after reading *The 7 Habits of Effective Leadership* by the late Stephen Covey Senior. It is pointless to focus on things we have no influence over. The same is true for holding on to something that is no more. You start with becoming aware, then you gain understanding of the situation, you actually see what is going on and how the disturbing thoughts have impact on you. In the end you can surrender by letting go and forgiving; both yourself and the other. In doing so, you create space for a new reality.

Letting Go

I will take you into a personal story about self-denial and letting go.

It was an evening in December, I had a business meeting to discuss my company. I can still picture myself in the reception room. Marc entered and with a firm exchange of handshakes we became acquainted. It seemed as if he held my hand for an unprecedented length of time and our gazes met. There was not much talk of business, it was personal and even emotional at times. That was the beginning of an intense and, for me, a complicated year. Marc was married and I was in a relationship, which I broke off shortly thereafter.

A year passed in which Marc took the time to make a choice for himself. After a year he finally left his home and family. For me, this was a difficult period and given the circumstances, a false start to an initially special encounter. I tied myself in knots trying to deal with the situation and placed myself in his shadow. In the meantime, he was busy living his own life, trying to get things back on track, and was struggling with a strong feeling of guilt towards his family.

I was looking in this relationship for a deep connection with myself and from there with Marc. I was the beaked whale who wanted to plumb the depths of the ocean, he was the dolphin who preferred to mostly play on the surface. His inclination was to go his own way; he loved his work and devoted his time to it, set the agenda, went on trips when he wanted to and forgot important things, including once my birthday. The latter hurt me terribly, I was ashamed and didn't dare tell anyone.

What I did do, was hold on to the potential I saw in our connection. I felt I had to work extremely hard to make 'us' work. My frustration came to a head after a few years, drained to the marrow as I was. I had been overexploiting my soul's desire for a long time and had lost myself. I lacked the safety to be relentlessly myself and to take up my space. It felt like my life had come to a standstill and this showed in my work and social life. When the bomb exploded and I threw in the towel, Marc turned his back on me and never looked back.

It became painfully apparent to me that I had wormed my way into a relationship in which I had become blind. I had settled for a connection that did not nourish my soul but rather eroded it. It was harrowing for me to realize how I had not taken responsibility for myself for a long time. I had allowed him to request I be positive, sweet, and cheerful and above all not demand any attention. Saying something about it was complicated, as I was then labelled demanding or jealous. Above all, I was the one who had denied myself, by being someone I was not and by settling for a place in his shadow.

It took a while before I could see the helplessness of two people who loved each other, but did not speak each other's language nor knew how to build a bridge. This is where acceptance and letting go started, as well as opening the door to more space, authenticity, and warmth in my life.

We tend to hold on to what is not good for us. Each human being has aspects in their life that form the common thread in their development path. Ask yourself what yours are. Are there certain areas in your life where you repeatedly face challenges? For most of us, there is an aspect that predominates, it could be in your work, or in specific collaborations, in family relationships, in friendships or perhaps in your home environment.

Letting go is crucial to free yourself and create room to move on. You don't for example let go of an assignment, of your company, your father or of a friend; that is outside of you. You let go of something that touches you from the inside. It is a deeper theme within you, which is really what it is all about.

Guidelines for Letting Go

1. Know what it is you want to let go of. Name what that is. Make sure that this is something that lies within you.

2. Do not associate with what you feel. You are not sad for example, you feel sad. It is the weight of your thoughts and feelings that make it heavy. Be aware of the words you use.
3. Give yourself time to let go and be gentle with yourself. Most people do not succeed in letting go from one moment to the next. Even if you do, you may find that the theme, the situation, or the person is still with you. Do not resist, let it be.
4. Distract yourself every now and then to stay out of your thoughts and to sink into your body. In this way you create space for the voice of your intuition. This could be working in the garden, cycling, walking, playing guitar or doing something creative. As long as it is something you can lose yourself in for a while.
5. Make the choice to let go, even if it does not happen from one moment to the next.

It is only once we have let go of something or someone, that we can open ourselves to new connections. I needed to see Marc again. He avoided meeting me for a long time, but after eight months we did. That confrontation was exactly what I needed. We had come full circle; it was a special and also emotional meeting. I was relieved to feel that things were right the way they were. I felt acceptance and was able to look at him, and his everlasting inner quest, with compassion. And that despite the fact that he had been in a new relationship for some time. It literally took me no more than two days to cut the link with him and I felt my heart opening up again. I am grateful for this experience because it has helped me learn to be relentlessly myself. Everything you experience, no matter how painful, brings you one step closer to yourself.

"Many people aspire to go to a place where pain and suffering do not exist, a place where there is only happiness. This is a rather dangerous idea. Without suffering, we do not have the opportunity to cultivate compassion and understanding; and without understanding there can be no true love." – Thich Nhat Hanh

The Wisdom of Non-judgmentalism

Judgments do not serve you in any way and have a negative effect on your energy and state of being. Being non-judgmental is an important theme in the context of letting go, as it has a great impact on how you look at yourself and how you relate to others. A life without judgment, how beautiful would that be. Is it a utopia? How many people manage to be truly free of judgment, starting with themselves but also towards others? We are often harshly critical of ourselves and it wouldn't be amiss were we to be a bit more lenient towards ourselves. So much for being non-judgmental towards ourselves.

There is an inner process one needs to go through before being able to be free of judgment towards others. The wisdom of non-judgmentalism is gained by getting to know your inner darkness. The moment you feel the darkness inside you, you lose all grounds to judge. A feeling of understanding and compassion arises, for yourself, for others and for everything around you. That is the source of the true understanding of love. Once you can forgive yourself, the need to judge, in whichever form, disappears. When you succeed, you liberate yourself from the ballast of judgments that oppress your heart. I will discuss forgiveness in more detail in the next chapter. Discover first how wonderful it is to free yourself from judgment and the blessing of being surrounded by people who do not judge.

Being Judgment-free

To help you on your way to being as judgment-free as possible, I am sharing an exercise with you that will help you become aware of the judgments you make about others.

Step 1 - Setting the intention

Start the day with the intention of being judgment-free.

Step 2 - Be alert for judgments

Spend a day focusing on being alert to the judgment behind everything you do. You will discover how beautiful this is, but also how difficult. The tiniest thought about someone on the street, walking just a bit too close or looking at you in a certain way or ignoring you, can prompt a judgment.

Step 3 - Choosing to let go

Only when you are aware of the judgments you make, can you make the choice to let go. Make this choice if it feels right.

- ∞ The process of acceptance is a life lesson and requires time and attention. Only time eases the pain, but it does not automatically take it away.
- ∞ Awareness and understanding are important conditions for change and letting go.
- ∞ When you make the choice to let go of something, know what it is you want to let go of. It is always something inside of you.
- ∞ Letting go is about releasing yourself from the load you are carrying and by doing so you create space to move forward.
- ∞ The trick is to take everything that comes and goes in life for what it is.
- ∞ If you can be grateful for everything in your life, you walk the path your soul has in mind for this life.

7

DISTANCING YOURSELF FROM WHAT DRAINS YOUR ZEST FOR LIFE

In the previous chapter I talked extensively about accepting and letting go. In this chapter I will elaborate further and pay attention to the things that can take away your zest for life and hold you back from being able to be yourself. The topics that will be discussed are surrender, trust and forgiveness. When we surrender to something, it means in fact nothing else than unconditional acceptance of what is. Trust is needed in order to surrender. Trust what you are doing is the right thing. At the same time, to trust, we also need the courage to fail and to surrender to what is. This requires that we stand firmly in our own center.

The moment you surrender, you stop resisting the situation and are prepared to accept whatever comes your way, whatever it may be. You are driven to surrender in situations where you see no way out. Some people have mixed feelings about surrender and perceive it as a sign of weakness. That is not the case at all. Surrender is going along inwardly with what is and no longer resisting whatever presents itself. You could say that surrender requires courage and character. This is also linked to trust, but I will come back to it later. I will take you through Michele's example.

Michele had been running her own business for a few years. She is great at her job, immensely dedicated, modest of personality and extremely likeable; loved by clients, colleagues and in her private life. At some point she was offered the opportunity to share her message on stage with a few hundred people. A request that touched on a burning desire of hers, but at the same time threw her back into feelings of disbelief and doubt. We had been working in the meanwhile for some time on getting her story clear. She found the invitation to speak exciting. It immediately galvanized and challenged her. It came at the perfect time and, after giving it some thought, she decided to say yes. Until recently, she had never thought she would be able or dare to do so. It is only once she could feel her unique added value in every fiber of her body, and that her story stood rock solid, that her confidence in the situation and the courage to take it on, grew. And it happened, she shone on stage. She managed to stay close to herself and to surrender to the moment. Her greatest lesson was to discover and feel that her value lay in her quality of being.

You may have heard the saying, 'A man often suffers most from the suffering he fears.' The moment you choose to surrender to a situation that is troubling you, you experience the relief of suffering no more. This is sometimes in small things. When you want to cancel an appointment because you don't feel well or are actually very tired for example. How many people put this off until the very last moment because they don't want to disappoint the other person? And in the meantime, they worry and walk around with a knot in their stomach. What happens when you trust that the other person will be able to accept this and not take it personally? That is having trust and not tormenting yourself unnecessarily with unconstructive feelings. At times it makes one wish we could switch off our thinking, our intellect; it would make life so much easier.

A friend shared the harrowing story of the period around the death of his father, James. James suddenly became seriously ill and his situation deteriorated rapidly. He was only fifty-five years old and in the midst of life. I never met James myself, but what this friend told about his father was heart-breaking. James regularly lost his temper, commanded everyone in the house about and was unfriendly. He would say, 'You can see I am ill, do something,' or 'Hurry up'.

He quarreled with everyone and everything making the last few months of his life dismal. James could not find peace and surrender to the inevitable, the approach of death. His resistance was fierce and frustrating for him, but especially for those around him: his family and the people who loved him. As I listened, I felt my friend's sadness and how intensely painful it had been for him, his mother, and sisters, and how this feeling was still like an open wound in his heart.

I wish it on everyone to be able to surrender and let go of life just before it ends. That is the ultimate feeling of trust that things are the way they should be. This is a choice we have as human beings, but it is not so simple for everyone. Sometimes the person's ego and frustration are so strong that the soul lets go. This means in fact that your soul gives up developing further in this earthly life. We always have after all, as human beings, free will, right until the very last moment.

> **Flow as a Form of Surrender**
>
> Being able to surrender is also an important aspect in the work context. Many people aspire to be in a flow in their work. This is a state of being that you experience when you allow yourself to be carried along by the natural flow that you are experiencing. This can manifest itself in many ways, in the deals you make, the opportunities that come your way without having to push hard for them. This can also be seen in the people who suddenly appear on your path, who travel with you, and customers who know how to find you. You create a state of flow by being in an ultimate state of *being*. It is doing what you love to do from your authentic power of being and your energy and not from your power of thinking, as it then quickly becomes contrived.
>
> Flow is a form of surrender and trust that you do not have to run after something but that, if you are in alignment with yourself, you will attract what is meant to be. The best indicator is that which is brought about by inspired action and in loving connection with yourself and your environment.

Life is not about working as much and as hard as you possibly can. The trick is to learn to slow down and from there discover what your natural cadence is, and how you can find out that things can flow organically. Doing so you achieve more by doing less, in your own way.

Self-confidence is an important factor in trusting, as

you read in chapter six. But trust requires more than that. It requires you to let go of control and accept there are greater forces at play than you alone, or we as humanity in general, can comprehend. Not everything in life can be engineered and people sometimes have delusions of grandeur by assuming that they are the architect and greater than the power and wisdom of Mother Earth.

Exceptional times, such as the COVID-19 pandemic, are an example of this and call on you to have faith and find peace within yourself. To trust that this is temporary, and that there is a lesson in it for everyone. Lack of trust, in yourself and in others, can rob you of your zest for life, but daring to fail and forgiveness are also important themes here.

Daring to Fail and Forgiveness

Some people are willing to leave the safety of the harbor but lack the courage to make a breakthrough. This is recurrent in many aspects of life. That so-called safe cage to offer security, which in reality only keeps us in an impasse. What does it take to break free from it? To wait until life chooses for you, until life intervenes?

'You are going to know failure if you're brave with your life,' says Brené Brown. Sticking your neck out means that you will take blows along the way. It requires you to be vulnerable, to do what is not scripted and to break out of ingrained patterns that get in your way. Hereby it is not a question of running the risk of possible failure. No, it is knowing that you will fail and yet not letting that stop you from taking steps and showing courage. That is taking responsibility and choosing to take on life.

"Forgiveness is letting go of the burden of judgment."
– Deepak Chopra

You have most probably heard someone say, 'I can't forgive him,' and maybe you have said or thought this yourself at some point. Things happen in people's lives that are sometimes hard to digest. They can be unpleasant and heart-breaking experiences that, as a human being, test you beyond belief in your capacity to not stay stuck in a feeling of remorse towards the other person. This can be anything, for example a business partner you have allowed to betray you, or a love partner you have allowed to hurt you.

Where surrender, which I mentioned earlier, applies to situations, forgiveness applies to people. Forgiveness is not (or no longer) holding someone accountable for their guilt or part they played, in the context in question. We forgive above all for ourselves, to free ourselves from the millstone that hangs around our necks until we have forgiven. By letting go, we create space for ourselves to plant new seeds and move on. By this I mean being able to give ourselves once more in a connection with others and to trust them. You do that for yourself.

Forgiveness is taking distance from the oppression of whatever holds you in its grip and deprives you of a zest for life. I take you along in a story related to this.

Emma was on holiday in Canada with her family. One rainy day, all members of her family apart from her died in a car crash. In a foreign country, a drunk driver on a two-lane road. Emma said she would have preferred to die with her husband and children because the pain and grief of missing her loved ones was unbearable. Finally, years later, after a huge struggle with herself, she found a way to forgive the driver. Emma was even able to see and feel compassion for this man and his situation. For her, this was the only way to break free and allow herself a life in which she could move on from the grief of missing her family. In this way Emma managed to allow some beautiful moments to happen again.

This story shows how powerful forgiveness can be. You can't erase the pain, but you do have a choice in how you want to go on with your life. There is a saying in Buddhism: 'To remain bitter is to drink poison and hope that the other person dies.'

Your lingering in your anger can also be a burden to others. Think of the example of father James who fiercely resisted his impending death. The impact on those around him was enormous, not to mention his inability to forgive himself.

You yourself are a participant in everything in your life, that includes that failed partnership, that conflict or that broken relationship. Turn the spotlight on yourself and see how you can change your own outlook.

> **Your Part**
>
> Think about a specific situation that is bothering you and that you are not happy about (yet). Bring to mind the person with whom you had or have a conflict or friction.
> 1. Name the context and your feelings about the person involved.
> 2. State what your part in the situation was or is.
> 3. What is still preventing you from forgiving the other person?

People have a wonderful gift, and that gift is resilience. Emma's story above demonstrates this. It is what enables us to get through the most terrible events in our lives and move on. This simply does not happen without a struggle. It requires utter surrender to what is, feeling the pain and the sorrow, and finally making the choice of how you want to continue living. How intensely difficult that may at times be. Some people go through things that make you wonder how on earth they can ever pick up the thread of their lives again. There is no standard answer to that, except that everything is possible. There is no forgetting painful experiences, but by healing you can reinstall balance and experience the light as well as the dark.

- ∞ You are compelled to surrender in situations where you feel there is no way out.
- ∞ Surrender is the inner yielding and absence of resistance to a situation.
- ∞ Trust requires allowing that there are greater forces at play than you can comprehend.
- ∞ Forgiving is not, or no longer, holding someone responsible for their part in the situation.
- ∞ Forgiving someone is above all freeing yourself from negative feelings.

PART 3
GET TO KNOW YOURSELF BETTER

8

BE GENTLE WITH YOURSELF

"So many people seem to struggle with being kind to themselves. If you don't have genuine love and kindness toward yourself, how can you extend these to others?"
– Dalai Lama

Being *relentlessly yourself* is based on gentleness towards yourself. In life, self-acceptance and self-love form an indispensable basis. Everything we do in life brings us closer to our core, the essence of our existence, which is our soul. By tackling the patterns and beliefs that often unnoticedly hamper our development, we can literally clean it up. In this way, you can see yourself as the person you really are. In this chapter I will discuss the importance of being gentle with yourself. This is the foundation for standing in the center of life, doing what you are meant to do and being able to view others with compassion.

One

There is only one who is always there for me, who always stands by me, who sees me as I am and who loves me unconditionally with heart and soul. Someone who lovingly and patiently gives me the space to express who I am, someone who always has my back, no matter what. Someone who sees me in my gentleness and inner beauty, someone to whom I say wholeheartedly 'yes.' That person is me.

Suppose you fully accept yourself for who you are. That you love yourself and allow yourself to be you, without embarrassment, restraint, or false modesty. That you are gentle with yourself and leave all forms of self-conflict behind you. Self-love, not everyone finds it easy to feel it and act upon it.

Your Self-image

It touches my heart to see how some people tie themselves in knots by systematically depreciating and not valuing themselves. By saying: 'I'm not good enough' or 'I can't do that' or by making themselves dependent on the approval or appreciation of others. It is the words you speak that stand for the life you live. People so often make themselves smaller than needed. Recently, I heard someone say: 'I just have a high school education, whereas my sisters all have university degrees.' It is the word 'just' hidden between the lines, which has a world behind it.

What makes it so poignant is that those who make these kinds of statements often do so on automatic pilot and no longer hear what they are actually saying, let alone realize what they are bringing about energetically. Every time you think or speak these words, you confirm a story that you have created yourself. Thus, you reinforce the feeling of self-rejection.

There are also people who have heard from home how

smart the other children in the family were. Where (both or one of the) parents explicitly mentioned how well their brother or sister did at school or in sports. These are all examples of seeds being planted in your system that are a potential danger to your sense of self-worth.

In order to be gentle towards yourself, it is important to be clear on what your self-image is. This includes all the positive and critical thoughts that you have about yourself.

Revealing Your Self-image
This exercise consists of a number of steps to uncover your self-image. One important condition is that you do not hold back or be ashamed. This exercise is only of value if you are brutally honest with yourself. You can use the download at www.evelienvanes.com/download.

Step 1 - Thoughts about yourself
What thoughts do you have about yourself? Mention positive things, but also what you do not enjoy and do not like about yourself. Write everything down, whether these are things you only think or also express. Take a few days for it and write down what comes up.

Step 2 - Disappointed in yourself
What disappoints you in yourself? For example, what do you think you should have achieved already in your work and in life when you look at where you are now?

Step 3 - Read out loud and share
Read aloud to yourself what you have written and feel what it does to you.
When you have done this, find your sister or brother, or a

> good friend. Then read aloud to them what you have written 'as if you were talking about the other person'. So you formulate everything in the 'you' form.
> What happens to you while doing that?

In the last step of this exercise, the chances are high that you fail to actually say these words out loud to someone else. So why do we do this to ourselves?

Let this exercise stimulate you to look at yourself with more gentleness. Let it be a trigger for moments when you catch yourself thinking harmful thoughts about yourself, so that you can call yourself 'to order'.

You have probably heard the following statement, 'Treat others the way you want to be treated yourself'. Jay Shetty, inspirer, author and once a monk, I once heard (in a video) reflecting on self-love in a striking way. Suppose you turn it around and say: 'Treat yourself the way you want to treat others.' The point is that we treat ourselves with love and respect and that this is the basis for how we treat others. This approach is based on the principle: first take good care of yourself and only then can you really show love and respect to others.

"Just when our self-esteem is hurting most, we go and damage it even further." – Guy Winch

Self-acceptance

When it comes to self-acceptance, we are our own worst enemy. Our thoughts about ourselves can sometimes be downright ugly, negative, and judgmental, more so than we would ever be towards others. Even towards people with whom we do not even have a natural click in the first place. This is quite something when you think about it, especially since often enough we don't even realize it and we do it all the time.

'Your only task in life is to believe in yourself,' says Kribbe. For me, this is the basis: self-acceptance, self-love, and self-confidence, so that I can from there, set out wholeheartedly on my voyage of discovery of life, giving it substance and meaning in my own way.

A woman's relationship with her mother plays an important role in self-acceptance. As Kohlrieser says: 'Having a secure base with a feminine figure, is a significant part of the path to full self-acceptance.' A father or a male figure is never an equal substitute. For men, the situation is somewhat different and the connection with a mother figure is especially defining for the way in which they can bond with both men and women in their lives.

Own Beliefs

The thoughts we have about ourselves are not random. We all have a past, and it has shaped us: our upbringing, the environment we grew up in, the people we surrounded ourselves with. We have created, based on the nurturing mentioned above, a belief about how we see the world, ourselves, and others. This core belief, a term also used in cognitive behavioral therapy, forms the basis of our image of reality. What makes core beliefs so tenacious is that you often carry them around for many years and they have become part of your script. Each person lives according to a script in which we have determined for ourselves what is 'true'. What you experience is often seen as a confirmation of your script. We tend to twist reality so that it fits our script and, in this way, we complete the circle and keep our core beliefs alive.

Leo is known for his sceptical attitude, whether it is a conflict at work, problems in his relationship, friction with friends or difficult contact with his son. He always manages to find somewhere, in everything that happens, confirmation of his scepticism. He says: 'You see, it's true.'

When I question him further on his scepticism, Leo appears to be convinced that people cannot be trusted. He is adamant about this and believes that people act, by definition, out of self-interest. In his view of the world, this is almost always at his expense. He sees everything that happens in his life as a confirmation of his core belief.

Leo sometimes says: 'I feel lonely.' His mistrust only increases his frustration with how many things in life go, and that in turn reinforces his sense of loneliness. The basis for being able to connect with others with an open heart and from a place of confidence, is affection, and that starts with loving yourself.

To break away from his core belief that nobody can be trusted, he will first have to become aware of the way in which this belief is a form of self-sabotage. Only then will there be an opening for him to slowly realize that the world and others do not need to change, but that the change lies within himself.

Leo's example is about trust, ego, assumptions, and presuppositions, but it is also fundamentally about self-acceptance and self-love. There is often an undercurrent sense of loneliness and insecurity and the behavior is an attempt to push it away. The problem is that, as in Leo's case, we are mostly not aware of what we are doing. Self-love is the key to a gentler view of oneself and of the world.

In order to break the cycle of the story you tell yourself and perpetuate, we need to understand where we acquired our core beliefs. The basis often goes back to our childhood. In my practice I see a lot of people stuck in their growth due to beliefs they inherited from their parents. These are often people in their forties and fifties who have been struggling for years but have not been able to turn it around, like Christy.

Christy has a mother who always resigned herself for the sake of others. She now suffers from Parkinson's disease and no longer lives independently. Christy visits her once in a while and still finds it confronting. Her father was a dominant and distant figure in the family. He was often absent, literally but also figuratively. Her mother hid behind him and was at his service. Her mother would, where possible, cover up all her father's irregularities vis a vis Christy and her two sisters.

After her studies, Christy met a man she fell madly in love with. A man she looked up to and – unsurprisingly – someone with the same dominant traits as her father. And what did she do? She faded to the background, just like her mother used to do with her father.

Christy kept this up for years, until a good friend became seriously ill and died soon after. This was a dire period which opened a cesspool of grief in her. It turned out to be a trigger for her to realize that she was living according to her mother's core beliefs and not her own. This insight was the beginning of a deeper process of realization that it was time for her to start living her own life. A life loose from her mother and back to herself and her own beliefs and life vision.

When it comes to self-esteem, it does not matter how successful someone actually is. In my work, I meet people who have an admirable track record but who nevertheless feel that they are not good enough. Or who work extra hard to live up to the image the outside world has of them. The things outside themselves seem important and take priority over what serves them. The ego is stubborn and sometimes difficult to recognize for what it is. More about this in chapter nine.

Recognizing Your Core Beliefs

Knowing what your core beliefs are is a good thing. Not everyone has them on the tip of their tongue. It is important to take the time to discover your beliefs. There are several things you can do to find out.

One of the ways I like to use, is to write. For me, writing is an extremely effective way to expand my awareness, to muse, to tune in, to ask myself questions and thus to come to deeper insights. I write just about every day in my journal, my thoughts, on how I feel, and what is going on deep inside of me. If writing is not your thing, you can also speak your story out loud and record it. There are also people who draw, paint, play music or have another creative hobby and in this way reflect and increase their self-awareness. It does not really matter which form you choose, as long as you find a way to express what is going on inside of you.

Another way to uncover your core beliefs is to ensure you have people around you who can hold up a pristine mirror to you. People who speak to you about what they see and feel free to confront you lovingly and unselfishly. For me, these people are worth their weight in gold in my life and I have learned to welcome them with open arms.

I regularly encounter people in my practice, who come to the realization that there are actually very few people in their immediate surroundings who stimulate and encourage them in their personal development. This is often because they themselves have changed and their social circle or work environment no longer fits. It is important to realize that nothing is cast in stone. People who are not in your life today may suddenly be there tomorrow. Every day offers opportunities for new encounters that can be crucial on your path. Trust that they will present themselves when the time is right, so long as you create movement and open yourself to it.

Self-confidence in Men and Women

Both men and women struggle with presenting themselves to the outside world with self-confidence. Many women search for the right way to combine their femininity, with decisiveness and the setting of boundaries. It is often quite a quest to find a manner to do so, that fits each individual. The outside world is quick to perceive it as exaggerated or contrived. Women can usually afford to do so less than men; when women are powerful, they are quickly seen as (too) business-like or sometimes even labelled as an *iron lady*. Moreover, women can't permit themselves to have as many bad traits as men. The norm is that women remain polite, behave in a socially desirable manner, and do not get angry.

As Stella Bergsma says, 'Traditionally, women still have to balance on a thin rope.' This is the stubborn reality. In that respect, self-confidence arising from the feminine energy has, in addition to an individual change, also a collective transformation to go through. The roots of this lie deep and transcend the woman in her individual development.

Women in particular have been taught it is good to be helpful, socially adjusted, and connective. And in the same manner, showing deviant behavior, thinking of yourself and being contrary are supposed to be bad and inappropriate. Many women feel they have to bite their tongue in order to comply with these roles, while that may not be in line with their nature. Saying yes when they actually feel no, out of fear of being judged or perceived as bad. The more you deviate, the more you are scrutinized. This is the world we have created together. Fortunately, a change is taking place in which people increasingly know who they really are, what the core of their being is, and have the courage to stand up for it.

As human beings, we all have male and female energy within us. The feminine energy of connection and love needs to be expressed in a self-aware way so that it serves a broader purpose than just the inner process. Acting powerfully and standing up for yourself is valid when it comes from love, empathy, and connection. Ideally, both men and women would be in harmony with the two energies, just as it is meant to be. Fortunately, nature helps in this as something happens in both women and men around their mid-life phase. I will come back to this in chapter twelve, where I look at the dynamics in different life phases for men and women.

Whatever your gender or sexual orientation, you are who you are, and you are entitled to have and show your authentic self, that unpolished side of you. This is what makes you human, unique in your being and worthy of your embrace, as long as you live life with respect and carry a warm and pure heart with you.

Self-love as the Basis of Self-confidence

'It is almost as though self-esteem gives a Teflon coating to the soul,' says Kohlrieser. Self-love is at the base of self-confidence. How beautiful would it be to look at yourself in the mirror with love, gentleness, compassion, and pride? Can you feel that you are perfect the way you are, inside and out, and can you feel that you matter? That you are a unique person, with a gift, and can you view yourself as valuable, for both your vulnerable and your powerful sides? That also means taking yourself seriously and listening to yourself.

When your self-image is good, you are able to recognize both your strengths and limitations without compromising your self-esteem and the feeling that you matter. Your resilience is then strong enough to hold your ground, whether you make mistakes or are criticized by others or not.

Self-esteem is also the foundation for looking at others with understanding. 'When you really immerse yourself in your being and when you develop understanding of your own humanity, your view of other people will soften,' says Kribbe. When you only focus on others and do not really take yourself into consideration, or love and accept yourself, what you do and think about others is a sham. The connection with yourself is the foundation for connecting meaningfully with others.

Being gentle with yourself moreover is the starting point for looking at others in their process, with kindness and without judging. You don't know the others' background or story, and therefore you do not know why they do what they do.

As we grow older, we tend to become milder and we also dare to be more vulnerable. We have the courage to be who we want to be and no longer feel the need to create a pseudo-version of our true nature. This is about self-love and the basis for having more compassion for those around us.

Self-esteem is an ultimate act of self-love and surrender. At the beginning of this chapter, you took a look at your self-image. What would happen if, from today on, you chose to stop torturing yourself with constant judging and negative thoughts about yourself? Instead, you choose only positive thoughts and words when thinking of yourself. When you stand in the bathroom in the morning, for example look at yourself for a minute, with gentle and loving eyes. Does it feel strange or uncomfortable? Then start with a smile or say something sweet or nice to yourself. Open your heart consciously and let the self-love flow. It may feel awkward, but go ahead and do it. Confront yourself to see who you really are in all your beauty and vulnerability.

Whatever happens in life, the value you have, your intrinsic value, is part of you and is always there to fall back on. There may be times when you feel less connected to it, but that does not mean your value has disappeared. It is always there, and you can always connect with it, no matter how difficult the road leading there may at times seem. It is merely your perception: when you are open to seeing it, it is there. This reminds me of the quote by the now deceased psychotherapist and author Wayne Dyer: 'If you change the way you look at things, the things you look at change.'

- ∞ We damage our self-confidence with our thoughts about ourselves.
- ∞ As human beings, we all have male and female energy, and the art is to balance both energies within ourselves.
- ∞ The basis of self-confidence is self-acceptance and self-love. Looking at yourself in the mirror and feeling love, gentleness, compassion, and pride for who you are.
- ∞ Self-esteem is an ultimate act of self-love and surrender.

9

A HEALTHY EGO

"The ego isn't wrong; it's just unconscious. When you observe the ego in yourself, you are beginning to go beyond it." – Eckhart Tolle

Success arising from a place of purity and as a contribution to the greater whole is beautiful, constructive and deserves more room to be. The ego has, besides a negative and destructive side led by the mind, also a friendly side that stems from the heart. In this chapter I will help you to distinguish between the two and discover how a healthy ego supports your success. It is all about daring to be who you are and not trying to make yourself bigger or smaller than you are.

Around the world you can see entrepreneurs shouting from the rooftops about their success, how wonderful their lives are and how, by following them, you can earn six-figures or more in no time at all. It has been a trend for years now, especially in online entrepreneurship, and appeals to the pursuit of wealth. Webinars in which people are called upon to shout out loud that they want to become millionaires.

We live in a society where the prevailing world view is that we stand out and get recognition when we are successful. Success and status are apparently the social bar by which we measure ourselves. In early 2015, I became active online with my coaching business, and I noticed many people were searching and craving financial success. So many searched for the golden egg, for passive income, for the fulfilment of a specific desire, for the stilling of their hunger. The question is: What are they really looking for? Many people find that their own fear and insecurity only intensify in the – at times blind – pursuit of financial success. There are also many who struggle to feel what is pure and what is not. I will mention two forms of unhealthy ego, starting with a large ego.

A Large Ego

The larger someone's ego, the more likely they have a lot of inner work to do. Even though we are all actors in a play, those who identify with their dream character – read their ego – are not aware that they are part of a play. As spiritual teacher and author Eckhart Tolle says: 'Every ego confuses opinions and viewpoints with facts and is a master of selective perception and impure interpretation.' By increasing your self-awareness, you can make the distinction from your heart, and not from your mind.

Fortunately, there are plenty of entrepreneurs, and I mean the *teachers* amongst them, who deliver a lot of value, are sincere, and feel an inner drive to help others. Yet there are also many who have not yet put their own houses in order and think they know the truth. It is also quite difficult to see through the large egos and distinguish the 'helpers from the false gurus', as Johanna Maria Riemen calls them. More books have been written about getting rich by people who are not rich themselves than by those who are. Be careful not to take-on things from *teachers* who are stuck in a large ego and have not yet healed themselves. I am reminded of a hilarious scene in the film *See No Evil, Hear No Evil* where you see the blind helping the deaf and vice versa.

There where it goes wrong for gurus, or wannabe gurus, is when they place themselves on a pedestal. Men and women who are dominant and high in their masculine energy often express their fear by lapsing into the extreme in order to prove themselves to the outside world. They busily create something from the outside that makes them feel good. In this way they remain stuck in their own ego system.

Someone standing on a podium can tell a passionate story and easily lead you astray with their emotions. When this is not genuine or founded on the soul, it is coming from the ego. The tricky thing is that the sender himself is often unaware that this is his false self, speaking. This means that someone does not necessarily have wrong intentions but is simply unaware and probably sincerely feels that this play is the truth.

Those susceptible to the stories of gurus who are stuck in their ego, are mostly searching themselves, and are still far from their true selves. The closer and the more grounded you are in your own authentic center, the clearer you can make the distinction between what is inspired purely from the heart and what is not. Ego and awareness are not two sides of the same coin.

The question is how you, as an observer, make this distinction. Observe the extent to which you perceive someone's ego. People with a large ego:
- Usually consider themselves very important
- Like to be the center of attention
- Are often dominant
- Show little modesty in the way they manifest themselves in company
- Can sometimes go too far in expressing *false modesty*

Think twice when you meet people stuck in their ego before you lose yourself in it. It is beautiful to feel compassion for someone's inner struggle and see that their actions are a result of inability and lack of awareness. You do not have to save anyone, just as it is not the idea that others save you. Accept that person for who they are, turn around and go your own way. When the time is right, that person will wake up and see for himself where he is trapped. There is moreover a danger that the other's subconscious will also get a hold on you. We must all take our own responsibility in life and you are allowed to protect yourself from the energy of people who are not good for you.

A Too Small Ego

I often encounter compassionate people in my practice, who want to do good for others, while ignoring themselves. These are the givers, the pleasers and caregivers who almost always put the other person first. A little healthy selfishness would not go amiss here. I remember years ago a friend telling me how his mother had changed after the menopause. He said she had always been there for others and that during and after her transition she suddenly took herself more into consideration. It took some adjustment from her environment, but I would say, 'good for her.'

Our life is not meant to only be at the service of others, leaving our own development to stagnate. Charity is beautiful, but not when it comes at your own expense. After all, that is going against your soul's plan here on Earth. Everything we do is in order for us to develop and learn, and to shake off the shells we have supposedly made our own. To return to who we truly are, to face our own reality, and that can be found in your soul.

I would like to offer you another stimulating perspective on the ego with this quote from McKenna, where he says: 'Wake up first, with pure and unapologetic selfishness, or you're just another shipwreck victim floundering in the ocean and all the compassion in the world is of absolutely no use to the other victims floundering around you. First resolve your own situation, and then you can maybe do something with your compassion that will help others.'

As you can see, there are several ways in which an overly small ego can also work against you seeing yourself for who you are and really being yourself. People with too small an ego:

- Hide behind others by excessively caring for or helping them
- Often ignore their own needs and interests
- Display extreme modesty
- Do not consider themselves important
- Are often highly insecure

Self-knowledge and the Ego

It is wonderful to see many children and young people within the new generation – many of whom new age children – who think differently and make a valuable contribution to the collective. By new age children I refer to those who show great intuitive awareness from birth or from a very young age. Younger generations tend to be less concerned with material things and are preoccupied from a young age with issues that many of today's generation of people in their forties and fifties only deal with around and after their mid-life stage. It is a matter of conscious thinking and feeling, of self-knowledge and of not going along with the crowd, but about steering their lives and the way they live from the inside out in a way that makes sense. This development will undoubtedly have a significant impact in changing the collective.

Achievement, self-reliance, and competition are the guiding principles in our self-created society. While many are busy avoiding vulnerability and focusing on material certainties, successes and emotional securities, there are increasingly more people who distance themselves from this. Who consciously choose to get more out of life and transcend the superficial level. It takes courage to dare to be vulnerable. To show yourself as you are and not pretend to be someone you are not. There is nothing you have to prove that you can do, or how strong you are, to anyone. Certainly not to yourself.

Everyone knows that life is not a continuum of merely happiness and a feeling of euphoria. Moreover, those who choose to live on the baseline will miss out on the lessons they could gain from these experiences. In doing so, they miss out on the insights needed to develop.

The zeitgeist we are currently living in, requires introspection and really engaging with life. As time moves on, more and more people are becoming aware of the importance of working on their mindset. This includes paying attention to the need to anchor new beliefs. You can influence yourself in a positive way by using affirmations, but make sure that you also work on your deeper feelings and be aware of what you are emanating. Make sure this is aligned with what you are telling yourself. For example: suppose you say to yourself 'I believe in myself' several times during the day, but do not actually believe it deep down. This then works counterproductively and strengthens your lack of belief in yourself.

Life is basically about feeling good, being your authentic self, feeling trust and inner peace, and not allowing fear and doubt to dominate your life. This is the foundation of a happy and successful life. Not really knowing who you are lays the ground for a troublesome ego, whether it is too large or too small.

Few people manage to stay close to themselves once they are on a certain career path. The feeling of wanting to uphold their status and success can lead to a yawning gap and keep them from themselves. This may manifest in the thought: maybe I should not do that as it could damage my career. Allowing yourself to be led by external recognition will sooner or later lead to disappointment. When your status and position are in the leading role, you are not in the pilot seat. This in fact also involves ego and is often unconscious. Even if the intention is pure, the driving force does not stem from the heart. This is the merry-go-round in which your actions can get you stuck.

Empowered Humility

People can easily become hostage to their own ego or vanity. Those held hostage by an arrogant attitude towards the world actually hide an underlying sense of inferiority and a lack of self-worth. In the book *Hostage at the Table*, Kohlrieser talks about empowered humility and the contrast with arrogance that is ego-motivated. Empowered humility is wanting to feel you are someone with a clear meaning and purpose. Someone who is driven to find significance from the depth of their soul and to manifest from there. Pure and authentic, without wanting to raise themselves above others and be filled with self-conceit.

Those imbued with empowered humility possess a convincing modesty, and do not seek public flattery. This is easy to recognize as they are usually rather unobtrusive, modest but amiable people. Therefore, empowered humility has nothing to do with low self-esteem, self-deprecation or a lack of self-worth. It is about feeling who you are, what you are and why you do what you do, while allowing others the space to do the same. Give some thought to whether you know people around you who fit this picture. These are particularly inspiring people.

> **Masculine and Feminine Energy**
> In the case of masculine energy, the extreme form of ego manifests itself as coercive, aggressive, and lacking

in empathy. Feminine energy can also manifest as jealous, manipulative, and hateful. When both masculine and feminine energy function at the level of ego, conflict and misunderstanding abound. On the other hand, when both the masculine and feminine energies function at the heart level, they are respectively protective, creative as well as heart-founded, loving, and connecting. Please note that we are talking about men and women here. Women also possess masculine energy and vice versa. There are plenty of sensitive men who do not feel at home in the flat one-dimensional traditional image of masculinity.

Your Driving Force for Success

Striving for success in line with the system we live by starts early in life: at school, during our years as a student and also when we start working. Success is an empty word until you give it meaning. It helps to understand how your ego influences your actions. I have previously discussed to this end, a large ego and an ego that is too small.

There is nothing wrong in itself with being successful and making good money, but know for yourself what drives you to do it. Is it primarily for personal gain, or are you doing this for a higher purpose? This is an essential distinction which determines the trueness with which you do things. If you say you want to earn passive income or become a millionaire, know what your deeper motive is. Be aware of what you are saying and whether what you think you want is a heart's desire or an ideal image that you have created.

Wanting success in combination with an ego-led drive, goes hand in hand with power and recognition. Success that serves only you and your own bank account will feel hollow and will not fill the feeling of lack or emptiness. This is called a *short-term rush* and will never contribute to fulfilment. Before you know it, the inner turmoil will quickly rear its head again. It is only once you are able to transcend and see through your own ego system, that you will understand that identifying with your ego leads nowhere. Your state of awareness will determine to a large extent how things will go for you, and therefore your business success.

Achieving success that is the result of pure intention, and which applies and makes use of your unique gift in life, will lead to emotional fulfilment. You will feel the difference in how this arises through relaxation and slowing down. You do your own thing, walk your own path, and do not get stuck on the merry-go-round. Should you manage to do so, then success will taste like a luscious fruit, the juice of which will drip from your mouth. Real success and meaning go hand in hand, one cannot exist without the other.

Defining success
1. What is success for you? Be as concrete as possible by really asking yourself how you feel about it.
2. Why do you want to be successful? What does it bring you?
3. What do you want to use your (financial) success for?

4. To what extent have you been successful in your work so far?
5. What made the above feel like success to you?

Choosing for Yourself

Liberation is found in choosing for life and for yourself, however difficult that may be. That starts with becoming aware of the subconscious and unconscious, in order to make other choices, free from the mantle of the ego. Satisfaction will never be found in living from ideal images. Just remember that on the path of your heart and soul there is no doubt, uncertainty, or inner turmoil.

When looking at what life is really about, knowledge and brain power get in the way of our journey of inner discovery. Knowledge, issued from our minds, lies outside ourselves and keeps us trapped in our heads and in our thoughts. 'Knowledge is precisely what stands between the seeker and the sought,' says McKenna. He uses the metaphor of the signpost on a long journey. No one thinks about the signpost itself. The knowledge that is needed on your journey of discovery will be there, when it is needed. Do not go searching for it too much as this shifts the focus from inside to outside, while here it is precisely your inner world we are talking about.

We have created the world we have ended up in together; a world mainly driven by rationality. That has inflated our ego and the illusions attached to it, and it is up to us whether or not to engage in it. Therein lies our free will. It is wonderful to see that people are increasingly wanting to break through this, by allowing their vulnerability to be and sharing what really lives within them.

Be aware of the extent to which you are in the grip of external pressures and allow yourself to be driven by your ego. 'The ego wants to control as it is afraid. The ego is constantly running around trying to save something, to save an image of yourself that you want to keep intact for the outside world,' says Kribbe. Control is an illusion. Measuring ourselves against unrealistic ideals of success and happiness, only lead us to become alienated from ourselves, from our core and moreover from our creativity. It is precisely our creativity that craves the space to move outside the box, to flourish uninhibitedly. This is only possible by going your own way and not letting yourself be held back by what should or should not be done.

> **Your Ego**
>
> Discover when your ego gets in the way and prevents you from being yourself. Notice during the next few days when your ego takes over. In doing that, keep the description above about a large and too small ego in mind.

Those trapped in a large ego cannot and do not want to objectively see what is going on and how they are entangled in their own ego. More often than enough they fail to see their negative patterns as negative and possibly even view them positively. When confronted with this by others, they prefer to keep them at arm's length or even put it back in the other's court. There are emotions at play here, but they only see them as deep feelings, which they are not. Those who do not confront the troublesome ego will feel a deep, gnawing sense of dissatisfaction inside and will not feel truly fulfilled in life.

The breakthrough lies in acknowledging the negative and troublesome ego and being open to those who want to confront them on this from a place of love. This, in practice, is a process that requires strong determination due to the unconscious nature of a large part of it. Nevertheless, there will be moments in everyone's life that offer a potential opening to a breakthrough.

How Your Ego Can Serve You

When we take this road of self-discovery, we not only serve ourselves, but also create the conditions to better see and understand others for who they are. It is the basis for being able to appreciate and respect others for where they stand. A healthy ego serves you by pointing out what is happening to you in connection with others. It helps you feel what is right and what is wrong and where you want to set your boundaries. A healthy ego enables you to see yourself as the person you really are, so that you can express yourself accordingly. That makes a healthy ego important, especially for women.

Take a look at people around you and observe their egos. See how for some people large egos have taken over and keep them away from themselves. Consider it a protection mechanism to avoid getting too close. By observing what happens to others, you help yourself to get to know your own ego better and discover when it serves you and when it does not. Your ego is also there to protect you, to keep you from pain and fear.

We have the free will to engage in something or not. It is also our free will to follow our ego that wants to protect us. Sometimes the pain and the confrontation are so intense, you doubt you can handle it. You do not have to if you don't want to and then you will not travel the deep valleys. It does mean however, that you are choosing to avoid the opportunity to deepen yourself, to expand your consciousness and give your life more meaning and fulfilment.

Take a look at your own ego and its dynamics. When does your ego protect you in a positive sense, in a way which is welcome? And when does your ego rear its end but you choose to follow your heart and thank your ego for its services?

- ∞ The closer you are to yourself, the clearer you can distinguish between what is inspired purely from the heart and what is not.
- ∞ That which gives the ego a *short-term rush* will never contribute to fulfilment.
- ∞ Emotional fulfilment is obtained by achieving success that is the result of pure intention, and the application and use of your unique gift.
- ∞ If you want to be successful, make sure you know what your underlying motives are and what you want to use your success for.
- ∞ A healthy ego serves you by pointing out what is happening to you in connection with others. By helping you feel what is right and what is wrong, and where you want to set your boundaries.

10

DISTINGUISHING TRUTH FROM REALITY

'The core of my being, is the ultimate reality,' says author Deepak Chopra. In the first chapter, I talked about our awareness as the core of our being, because without awareness, we have no lived consciousness of our being. You could say that without awareness, we as humans do not exist. The core of your 'being', your consciousness, is your reality. In this chapter, I will elaborate on what truth and reality are, and how they determine how we live our lives.

We often presume that others see exactly what we can see, but that is an assumption. The way you look at the world around you determines your perception of reality. Your thinking is not part of this and only hinders your perception. Every human being is different, and I am not talking about your personality or external characteristics but especially about your level of consciousness and perception. In that sense you could say that reality in a generic sense, does not exist. What does, is your perception of what you see, or think you see and feel.

To what extent do you ever put to the test what others observe? I was in the forest not so long ago with colleague entrepreneur Susan. It was a sunny day and after a walk we settled down on a huge tree trunk in a beautiful clearing in the forest. We sat there for a while, walked around, and gazed at the gigantic trees around us. I was impressed by what I saw and felt humbled by my awe of nature. At one point I asked Susan: What do you perceive here? This opened the way for a wonderful conversation on our perceptions. It is then that you discover how difficult it actually is to take someone else with you into the world you experience, to share and describe exactly what you observe.

You have your sight with which you perceive, your smell, your hearing, what you taste and what you feel. You could call these the five classical senses that play a large part in determining what you ultimately perceive, but it actually goes beyond these five basic senses. There are other filters. To start with there is a filter before light, vibrations, energy, and molecules reach our senses. Our senses then send signals to our brain of where the sensation took place, which constitutes another filter. The interpretation we give it and the words we use are a third filter. Our beliefs and patterns influence the words we choose. In short, reality and truth are highly subjective.

You will recognize what resonates with you. We can only perceive and consciously use that which corresponds to our inner level of development and frame of reference, which in turn resonates with our level of consciousness. 'We create our personal reality through our awareness, our decisions and actions, and that is only a small part of the all-encompassing, absolute reality,' says Christina von Dreien. Moreover, the patterns in our subconscious influence what we think we perceive. This prevents us, for example, from perceiving with an open mind. The triggers that led us to adopt those patterns, blind us in our ability to perceive.

There is No One Truth

There is no one truth, not even in science. The greatest scientists have been those who have looked at life from a more holistic perspective, such as Darwin, Einstein, and Tesla. Thinking in terms of measuring and knowing has become widely accepted in our society. As Antoine de Saint-Exupéry wrote in *The Little Prince*:

"Grown-ups love numbers. When you tell them about a new friend, they never ask the most important thing. They never ask, how does his voice sound? What games does he like the most? Does he collect butterflies? But they ask: How old is he? How much does he weigh? How many brothers does he have? And how much does his father earn? Only then do they think they know him."

It costs me more and more effort to talk with people who reason from a purely scientific point of view and for whom belief in science is absolute. Having a multidimensional view of the world is crucial for me. This means a holistic view of the world and of people, and I integrate this with my consciousness, understanding of myself and my role in the greater whole. I hope, and at the same time I know, that we are moving towards a future in which science and spirituality will go hand in hand and that this will be an enrichment for us and our children's future. By spirituality I mean the inner process of developing consciousness, being actively engaged in your individual development. It is about learning, deepening and the ability for personal growth. For there is so much more than the earthly reality, the perspective considered by many to be the reality.

That change is coming and is already in motion. If you stop to think, for example, about the existential questions around how humanity arose and why we are here. These questions simply cannot be answered via the scientific path. I find the prevailing materialistic view does not do justice to our existence. Life and the emergence of mankind on Earth is so magical and ingenious that it can hardly be a coincidence.

Our Scripts Color Our World

Everything around us is in fact fundamentally neutral. We are the ones who give it color, and that color comes from the script we live by as our beliefs about what is true for us and what drives us are anchored within it. We all live according to the stories we constantly tell ourselves.

Eric Berne, a Canadian psychiatrist and founder of transactional analysis, calls the self-fulfilling prophecy a life script. The choices we make in our lives become a script. Many people's thoughts tend towards the negative and this creates a script 'that turns into an ongoing, unfulfilling outcome – a negative self-fulfilling prophecy'.

Your stories have taken root in your thinking and acting, and this removes the open-mindedness with which you perceive. How often do you realize when talking to someone that your thoughts have run away with you? We are often preoccupied with ourselves and what is going on inside of us. The film we play drowns everything out and prevents us from sensing what is there in the moment. Perhaps you are thinking, 'he must have meant that...' or, 'the last time he asked that he meant that...'

You have most probably been in the situation where you are talking to someone and they look away and lose interest. It is disastrous for the connection and it can also make you feel really dismal. Many people have so much going on inside that they struggle to remain in the moment. That does not necessarily say anything about you as a person.

Real attention is therefore scarce; it requires an unbiased and open mind and the ultimate ability to be in the here and now. I also call it the neutral zone in order to be present without prejudice and open to the other. Deepening occurs when your attention is in the present. When you continue to ask questions and remain within the other's story and truly open your heart to what they are sharing. Hence the importance of knowing the triggers and pitfalls that form the script that you live by and that determines everything about how you live your life and how you relate to others.

Rewriting Your Script

We all tell stories to ourselves and to the outside world, and we do so according to our script. We formed this script somewhere in our lives, and little by little we polish it with the experiences on our path. As a child, you grow up in a family with parents or guardians who have certain views, beliefs, and opinions. You will have beautiful memories, but sometimes also tough moments and painful situations. In short, a multitude of information that you will have colored in, in your own way, and stored. This is what forms the foundation of your perception.

Friends, colleagues, and other people around you will also have an influence on who you are, how you think, how you live and on your script. 'You are known by the company you keep,' is something you will probably have heard said before, possibly in slightly different words.

It is likely that someone who has just seen a partnership fail, will have had enough and not want to enter into any more collaborations for the time being. Our experiences affect our perception of what is 'true'. By consciously learning from the things you experience, you ensure that you break free from previous experiences. It is, after all, an experience and in no way a template to how future collaborations will go. By recognizing what you could have done differently in the cooperation itself, and by integrating that into how you approach new encounters, it is feasible that you will enter a new cooperation in a different way.

Creating a new image of reality is by no means easy, but where there is a will there is a way. This new image of reality starts with stripping away everything that shrouds what really is. Important in this is that you uncover the roots of the past experiences that influence your perception. This means seeing and removing patterns, programming, and stories that you have made your own. Acuity will be required to get rid of everything that is not real, but merely a created image. Unlearning this (some call it detoxing) can destabilize you for a while as you are letting go of something that has been your foothold for a long time. At some point in life, we actually have less new things to learn, but we mostly have to unlearn things.

In order to rewrite your script, it is important therefore to be aware of what is in your script. This can be with regard to people in your environment, but also to organizations, nature, politics, in fact everything that you observe. Suppose you are in a business meeting in which there is a heated discussion, and it does something to you. What exactly happened and what is the story you make of it? Or think of a conversation with your partner which triggers something in you. But it can also be a message you received from someone which evokes a certain feeling in you. What story do you put together around it that goes beyond the facts? Every moment of every day offers a multitude of situations to examine your beliefs, assumptions, and the stories you tell yourself.

> **Awareness of Your Script**
> A good start to become aware of your script is to keep a log for a week, in which you reflect daily on the things you do and the thoughts and attitudes you have about them. Write this down using concrete examples. If you want to do this well, it will take some work, but it will provide you with many insights.

Indeed, some things you can only see from a distance. All change begins with awareness and understanding, and from there you can let go of the story and create a new script.

Finding your own truth is done by connecting to yourself, by slowing down and coming to terms with who you are. You cannot do that when moving at high speed and without distancing yourself from the noise around you. Slowing down is the key to open the gate to your inner world. You come to yourself in the silence, the peace and the vacuum and there you find your own truth. This can feel uncomfortable. Your ego and ingrained patterns will rattle at the door to disturb your peace. This is where the ultimate challenge to take it on begins. I will come back in more detail to slowing down in Part 4 and what it can mean for you.

"Stillness is actually another word for space. It has no form, and therefore we cannot become aware of it through thought. You are never more essentially, more deeply, yourself than when you are still." – Eckhart Tolle

Seeing the Other

Being relentlessly yourself sounds so much simpler than it actually is. Just as we have a filter in how we look at ourselves, noise arises in contact with others due to the images we have created. We often use our own imagination or desire when interpreting the image of others. This holds us back from seeing the other as he really is. Tolle says thereafter: 'A range of conditioned patterns of behavior come into effect between two human beings that determine the nature of the interaction. Instead of human beings, conceptual mental images are interacting with each other.'

When you look at relationships, more often than enough we are tempted to partly color in ourselves the image of our partner to make it fit what we desire. Don't we all want to believe in the feasibility of certain relationships, even though deep down inside we know better? It is not easy to admit this and yet it is the only way to avoid denying ourselves.

The art is in being yourself in connection with others, and in return seeing others as they are. 'It is no surprise that there are so many conflicts in relationships. There is no real relationship' says Tolle. What he means here is that many relationships, of whatever kind they may be, are in fact built on quicksand. This quicksand is a symbol for the mental images that have nothing, absolutely nothing, to do with who you are and who the other is.

Check in with yourself to see to what extent you do this in practice. Can you see the other person as he really is, without letting your wish or fantasy add colors of its own? You can save yourself a fair deal lot of misery by paying attention to what is, by being aware of the image you have of yourself and of how it influences your actions.

- ∞ Your reality is the core of your 'being'.
- ∞ The way you look at the world around you determines the reality you perceive. Your thinking is an obstacle to your perception.
- ∞ We can only perceive and consciously use what is in line with our inner level of development.
- ∞ Being aware of your script is the basis for looking at everything around you in a different way.
- ∞ It is within stillness that you come to yourself and find your own truth.

∞ Just as we have a filter in how we look at ourselves, our beliefs and conceptions influence how we look at others.

11

GETTING CLOSER TO YOUR TRUE SELF

A job that costs more energy than it brings, a social circle that feels more like social pressure than bearer of joy and energy. A work partner with whom you have found a modus vivendi but just does not really feel right. A pretty good relationship but one that doesn't make your heart sing. There are so many ways in which we can become more or less alienated from ourselves. In this chapter I will discuss becoming estranged from yourself and how you can delve into your inner self, get closer to your true self and make space for you to be.

Sometimes, we allow, against our better judgment, things to weigh on our hearts or make us feel down. We often know somewhere deep inside that it is not right, but we do not do what we should do with what we feel and know.

Knowing that something doesn't feel right is one thing, finding the courage to face it and break through is another. It is actually quite remarkable how this works, knowing and feeling something, but still leaving it for what it is, because for example it is too much hassle to deal with it. The question is: aren't you deceiving yourself? The security you think you have, is that not a false security? And how does the fear of the unknown relate to the fear of nothing changing? People get stuck out of fear of the unknown in many situations and then push their feelings away, hoping that the issue will resolve by itself, like Amy did.

Amy is forty-six and lives with her partner in a lovely house in a wooded area. She loves walking and cycling and walking with the dog. Amy works hard and has her own company. Her social circle is large, she still has many friends from her student days whom she sees a few times a year. She is fond of working in the garden, but hardly gets around to it. She feels that something is wrong somewhere, but she doesn't know what to do about it. She really likes her work and is dedicated to it. She feels that taking a step back is not an option for her.

There are plenty of things in her life for which she is grateful: a successful business, a good and loving husband, three sons who are doing well and a wonderful place to live. And yet there is something eating away at her through the almost constant tension she feels. The sensation of continuous pressure, from her clients and from maintaining all social contacts, of which there are many. Her me-time is structurally compromised, and she struggles with that. Personally, she believes she has no reason to complain: 'I have everything a person could want, don't I?' As a result, she keeps on going.

In the meantime, it has been about three years since Amy went through a period in which she was regularly overtired. She was often sick, had a cold, inflamed sinuses, but she continued to work though still unwell. When she gave in to it, sometimes she had only just recovered when something else would turn up. She struggled in this way for years. It is only once her husband insisted that things could not go on like this, that she reluctantly realized that there needed to be a structural change. She realized that this was not the life she wanted to live.

Amy's example reminds me about the impact of a lengthy dormant situation. In this way, the constant drip of water is powerful enough to erode stone. Amy's story above is telling of how an apparently innocent situation can in fact be a real killer. Like hidden appendicitis causing a nagging pain that cannot be breathed away. It is only when the pain or the gnawing feeling returns repeatedly, that an opening arises to do something about it. The *law of free will* then prevails. Nobody will tell you that you that you have to face 'it', but this law implies that you bear the responsibility for the consequences of the choices you make.

The desire for true joy in life must be that much stronger for you to take the plunge. This is in fact also a form of being stuck in your ego, which leads you to maintain something that is not really there because it is not in line with who you really are. I can feel compassion for those who do not really dare to take on life. It is not the easiest way to confront yourself with what is going on deep inside. To follow suit and admit that this is not the life you want to live after all.

Live by What is Really Important to You

"Every man is two men; one is awake in the darkness, the other asleep in the light." – **Khalil Gibran**

The majority of people who have become estranged from themselves are not aware of it. I call them *the dead among the living.* We all have, in some way, phases when we are not awake. We often think we know ourselves, but it turns out to be based on the script that we live by and keep repeating. Many people live from day to day and do their thing. Even when they sense somewhere a nagging feeling of unease, they continue on the same footing and live life as they are used to. Maybe assuming that this is life and that, whatever you do, there will always be a gnawing feeling of inner turmoil.

A closed heart and a lack of 'being able to feel' will never lead to joy and fulfilment. It is not for nothing that life sometimes intervenes with triggers and impactful events. Circumstances that can be violent in the moment but come with the opportunity to learn from them and bring the underlying message to the surface. In such a way that you can make different choices and give your life a deeper meaning.

The reality is that we all have moments when we push away, against our better judgment, certain impulses or soul nudges. This is what makes us human and it is also a challenge to be constantly *on par* with ourselves. It is however a choice to structurally settle for a life that is not right for you. Why would you do that?

It pains me to see people trapped in themselves, who you feel and know will regret on their deathbed not having done what they really wanted to do in their heart of hearts. Your deathbed is not the place to start seeing that. Whether you are thirty, fifty or seventy, it's better late than never to take on life. In Dutch there is an expression that says: 'Life is a party, you just have to hang the streamers up yourself.' I understand the intention behind that statement well, it is up to you to make something of it. For me, however, this goes a step further. Life sometimes means working hard on yourself to grow in consciousness and give your life meaning and fulfilment. If you do that, it will give you true joy in life and that goes beyond hanging up the streamers.

Life is a unique gift that many people do not know how to handle. It takes courage to really embark on life's journey of discovery; the journey of self-discovery. The path of least resistance is blissful and that is an important principle, both in business and in other areas of your life. Nevertheless, there are periods in which we feel we are sailing full steam ahead with wind force six. That, too, is life.

Years ago, I read *The Top Five Regrets of the Dying* by Bronnie Ware, an Australian author and speaker. The book written as a result of her work in palliative care. In it, she shares the top five things people regret on their deathbed.

1. I wish I'd had the courage to live a life true to myself, according to my own values and insights, and not the life others expected of me.
2. I wish I hadn't worked so hard.
3. I wish I'd had the courage to express my feelings.
4. I wish I had stayed in touch with my friends.
5. I wish I had let myself be happier.

Let these top five encourage you to do things differently so they are not the words you speak on your deathbed. Thereby it is not so much a goal in itself to pursue happiness. It is the absence of the urge to 'be happy' that is at the source of true happiness. The search for happiness is essentially the search for ourselves, for who we are at our core.

"The best time to plant a tree was 20 years ago. The second-best time is now." – **Chinese proverb**

> **Your Time and Attention**
> Consider how you live your life and ask yourself the following questions:
> 1. What do you give the most time and attention to?
> 2. What would you like to pay more attention to? And why is that?
> 3. What is stopping you from doing that differently today?

Clearing Out

It is valuable to know what you want to do differently in life. We may to this end, more often than not, let go of what no longer serves us. Clearing out can be done by literally sorting out your house, your belongings, and your clothes. Many of the things and clothes that we have, have not been used for ages. Everything that you hoard, which has no use, function or meaning, is ballast that you carry with you. By getting rid of it, you create space, both literally and mentally.

You can also clear out your entire system. This has a huge impact and is about breaking patterns, which are sometimes passed on from generation to generation and have become part of your system. Every human being has ruts from the past and it takes time, attention, and space to bring them into focus. We have anchored these ruts into our system as if they were part of our 'being'.

These ruts often transcend the earthly life we are now

living and go back far in time. Think of themes that also ran through previous generations in the family line. These can be old traumas that trickles down through generations. Sometimes you run into themes that you cannot trace back to your own life. It is then very likely that they go back further, which does not mean that these traumas cannot be healed.

Traumas exist to be healed, so that their burden is not passed on to new generations. Should you feel the need to heal family traumas, then take a look at them with an expert, how for example a (family) constellation can help.

- ∞ The majority of people have become estranged from themselves and are not aware of it.
- ∞ Many realize on their deathbed that they have not lived the way they would have liked.
- ∞ Clearing out your belongings and your system allows you to let go of what no longer serves you.

12

INNER GROWTH

Let me walk my path, let me fall and rise again, let me learn about life, about myself, about the dynamics of high peaks and deep valleys. Let me make my own choices, even if they do not always turn out the way I intended. Let me live my way, by being who I am. Let me take a little bump, stumble, break my leg. Let me love intensely, connect with people, and then go my own way if that is better. Let me know pain, feel sadness, and experience that earthly life is not always fun. Let me discover who I am, ask myself over and over again who I truly am and find my way to dare be relentlessly myself. Let me be true to myself and to my soul's desire. Let me dive to the ocean's depths to discover what life is really all about. Let me be pure, with that rough edge. Let me be angry, be passionate, be playful, act crazy and be mischievous, let me cry and laugh. Let me discover why I am here. Let me take on life the way I do. Let me BE.

Being who you are is the starting point of everything in life. It is the movement from inside to out. In this chapter I will discuss what is important in this process. It is about inner growth and seeing yourself as you really are. This is a clear knowing or clear feeling of who you are at your very core, arising from your heart and soul, and you will need to work on this at different phases of your life. I also help you to discover how your body can assist you in being more in touch with your feelings.

"In the sea there are countless treasures, but if you desire safety, it is on the shore." – Abu Sa'id

Each human being is on this Earth for a reason. You would otherwise not be here. We can all choose to discover our life purpose, and each phase of life has its own dynamic in this. Moreover, the things we experience and the people we meet on our way, play a part in this in one way or another. They are there to mirror us, to show us the way and sometimes to confront us because taking another path seems a better choice. Persian Sufi and poet Abu Sa'id once said, 'Each soul is created for a purpose and its light is lit in that soul.' It is up to each person to discover this. To discover means to search, to ask questions, to feel, to look critically at yourself and to take risks.

'Inner growth does not happen by itself, unfortunately it is not a "natural" process,' says Johanna Maria Riemen. It requires dedication and honesty towards yourself and if something is really important to you, you will make sure that you make time for it.

If we take the metaphor of nature: animals, insects, know how to feed themselves, how to live and survive by hunting and using their instincts. Each soul has this in them by nature, both animals and humans alike. Your instinct allows you to react immediately. It is man and animal's mechanism to defend and protect themselves when for example faced with a threat.

Nature is endowed with faultless wisdom. Nature teaches every soul, including animals, how to seek their destiny. Should the soul fail to take this up, fail to see or awaken to it, this is not due to nature. Nature keeps calling, just as our environment keeps mirroring and calling. According to Sufi founder Inayat Khan, where we differ from animals is: 'Man was not born on Earth to eat, drink and sleep, but to learn how to best make use of this fertile soil.'

The responsibility for being who you are is always yours, even though you will encounter situations and people in your life that will put this to the test. This could be a partnership that does not flow, a friendship that is out of balance or a struggling love affair. Whatever the situation, the question is, what is it that you do to turn the situation around so that whatever is stagnating can flow again.

Sometimes you yourself need to change in order to remain yourself. Do you often find yourself in situations where you wonder how you got there? Then ask yourself why this happens every time. There is apparently a lesson to be learnt. At times the message will be harsh, but necessary for you to awaken. It could be for example, because the situation gives rise to feelings of injustice or because you wonder why someone treats you this way. You are the one allowing it and maybe not setting enough boundaries. Or you do not surround yourself with people who give you the space to be who you are. People who love you give you room to be yourself. This applies to both people in your work environment as well as in your private life. You want to be surrounded by people who feed your soul.

It is often the moments of crisis that reveal who we are

and how well we know ourselves, know our souls. Your soul is 'the most precious thing we have been given, which we must rediscover', according to Riemen. The soul is our *being* when everything that clouded it has been cleared away.

Using Time Gifts

We live in an era in which people are increasingly wondering what they want as they feel that something is missing. This is reinforced by the current pandemic and leads to some people feeling lost, bored, and as if walls are closing in on them. Boredom however is nothing more or less than denying yourself space to let your creativity flow. As a child, I was sometimes bored on Sundays. I had had gymnastics in the morning and my parents would play 'Sunday music' in the afternoon. I would then retreat to my room and often unleash my creativity.

> 'Time gifts' are what Christina von Dreien calls the moments in our lives when we suddenly have time and a chance to look more closely at ourselves. If, for example you unexpectedly lose an assignment and have to sit at home, lose your job, become ill or suffer from burnout. These are all opportunities to turn inwards and work on yourself, instead of looking for the solution on the outside. This requires trusting that what happened was not for nothing and that it also offers possibilities and opportunities. Instead of immediately suppressing the chaos in your head, it is good to let it simmer for a while and find your way through it. Just let the discomfort

> momentarily sit there. And maybe reading this book is also a 'time gift' for you. Let it do its work.

When you allow yourself to playfully discover your next step, new doors will open to you. For this you will need to create movement by taking inspired action. Let your creativity flow from within and remember what I mentioned earlier about nature and the animal kingdom. This is also a matter of going for it, discovering and gradually unveiling the intention. It is the movement we make from within that brings clarity and changes our view of what lies beyond us.

I hope that the day will come when children learn more about life at school, about what is needed to take it on. Learn tools on how to be yourself, how to recognize when you become alienated from yourself, how to deal with conflicts, how to make choices in a way that suits you, how to learn to listen to your heart, how to hear when your intuition is speaking to you. About learning to love yourself, connecting with others and learning to listen with attention. And what it means to stay true to yourself, to know what you want and why, to dare to speak out and to stand up for who you are. Managing to organize education in such a way that these kinds of issues were addressed would save a lot of therapy and coaching later on in life. It is not for nothing that there are so many coaches and that this number is only growing. For many of them this is only a temporary whim to deal with their own themes.

Stages of Development

There are different phases in your life and in your journey of inner discovery. Barbara Hand Clow writes extensively on this in *Liquid Light of Sex*, a must read for anyone wanting to understand more about life and open to the wisdom of the universe, the planetary system, and its influence on humans from the moment of birth. I shall briefly outline the crucial stages in your soul's development.

We hit puberty around the age of fifteen. Some experience this more intensely than others. Puberty is a phase in which we as children become aware of the polarities within us, and this often does not happen in the most subtle of ways. It is a phase of discovery, of pushing back frontiers and of uncertainty, while at the same time you are also expected to make important choices for the future. There are some people who, because they more or less held off puberty in their teens, suffer the after-effects later on in life. A process of catching-up what should have occurred earlier is then set in motion.

It is only many years later, around the age of thirty, that who we really are crystallizes. By then we have detached from parents, guardians, and their influence, and have formed our own opinions and pretty much arranged our lives. Many have, by that time, their own house and have possibly started a family.

Thereafter, a few years before the age of forty, our midlife phase can begin. This period can continue until around the age of fifty. It is often a period of intensity that some people experience as a real earthquake. In this life phase we are ready to remember our story and discover our unique potential. This phase is crucial and decisive for discovering what you want.

Around the age of fifty, a phase begins in which the right and left hemispheres learn to integrate better. The duality between body and mind is healed. This phase of life usually offers more inner peace to those who took on life in previous years and have come to the core of who they are. Those however who fled from themselves will still encounter themes and traumas that can make their life turbulent. In a nutshell, the fruit you can reap in this life phase is determined by the extent to which you dealt with your 'shit' in previous phases of life.

Let us now take a great leap to the eighty-fourth year of life, which is on average the last period (twice midlife). In this phase, the evolution of our consciousness is complete. This of course also depends on the lessons that a person took on in life or not.

Midlife Crisis

A midlife crisis is never easy, but it is even harder when you resist the change. It is the most intense phase of personal evolution.

Men tend to find, during their midlife phase, that they want to bring the softness and feminine energy within themselves to fruition and balance it with their masculinity. To this end, they are inspired and nourished by their mothers, lovers, and daughters. Nature works in such a way that their feelings overwhelm them more and they cannot help but open their hearts. This is also called the *kundalini rise*, the energy that moves in our body from the lower chakras to our heart and above.

For women, the midlife phase means allowing themselves to create time and space to further develop their inner masculine aspects. In concrete terms, this means that they feel a need to express themselves more and to tap into their inner strength. This is harder in practice as many women have by then often experienced resistance to their potential power in their contact with men, such as their father, brother(s) and other men. Breaking through this is crucial, but then in a way the woman finds authentic and natural.

The midlife phase is often accompanied by physical symptoms that are all linked to the opening of the different chakras by the *kundalini rise.* Statistics show for example that men between the ages of thirty-eight and forty-four experience a remarkably high rate of heart attacks. This is an interesting fact as this is exactly the life stage in which they call on their hearts to open further.

Many men struggle to open their hearts and embrace their emotions, it renders them vulnerable and insecure. You often see, with men who find this hard, that the ego takes over and wants to rule and manage life from the head. Clow says: 'What is envied in another at mid-life reveals that which is desired the most.' The projection of what we see in others can be considered a valuable source of information. In negative terms this could be called jealousy; but positively speaking, it is what you would like to welcome into your life.

Knowing how the stages of life can accelerate your development can help you to go with the flow of life and surrender to what presents itself. The key is not running away from it.

Inner Child Meditation

This meditation exercise, inspired by Jay Shetty, is a powerful exercise that can help you in no time, get to the core of who you are, who you want to be and of your soul's desire.

Step 1 - Your younger self

Sit down in a quiet place where you will not be disturbed for the next fifteen minutes. Close your eyes, place your feet in a relaxed manner next to each other on the floor, preferably bare foot or in socks. Take five minutes to relax and feel if you are comfortable. Scan your body, as it were, from bottom to top, paying attention to each body part.

When you are ready, imagine yourself standing or sitting in front of your seven-year-old self. You are in the house where you lived at that time and take a moment to really see the house, the surroundings and yourself as a child. When you have reached this point, draw closer to yourself as a child, by for example holding or hugging yourself. Do this with all the love, warmth, gentleness, and compassion your heart can summon. Allow yourself to be carried away by the feeling and love for yourself as a child in those days. Imagine holding yourself as a seven-year-old, holding his or her hands in yours and remaining in each other's presence and energy.

Now look at your younger self and ask the following question: 'What is it that I am no longer doing which makes you upset or sad?' You are asking your younger self for advice. Keep asking and take your time to let the answer bubble up.

Then thank your younger self and give yourself a hug. Come back to yourself in the here and now and take a few long deep breaths in and out, repeat this a few times.

Step 2 - Your older self
Now imagine you are sitting opposite an older version of yourself, the image of yourself at eighty.
Hold the hands of this elderly version of yourself, see how the hands are marked and weathered and then look your elderly self in the eyes. What do you feel?

Then ask yourself the following question: 'What will I regret not having done in my life?' Leave the older version of yourself the time to answer the question. Leave the response time to come to you. Even if you do not get the answer right away, trust that it will come, now or later. Be patient.

You lovingly thank the older version of yourself and take a few more deep breaths, deeply in and slowly out. Gently open your eyes and take the time to return to yourself. Write down what you felt and saw during the meditation. Should you receive more insights later on, then add them.

"We don't stop playing because we grow old; we grow old because we stop playing." – George Bernard Shaw

Getting in Touch with your Feelings

Not being in touch with your feelings (anymore) is a sign that you have strayed far from yourself. It may sound confrontational, but that is how it is. As Chopra says: 'The only way to feel is to go deep enough into yourself.' If you struggle to be aware of your feelings, there is a good chance that you have been denying, muffling, or suppressing your emotions for a long time. You often see people who are struggling to access their feelings, compensate in matter. Their self-worth and identification are then derived from things, prompted by their intellect, which can be a nice car or a gadget.

Sometimes people find themselves in circumstances that feel like 'survival', where they think they have no options, no choice. Whatever happens in life, we always have a choice. Taking refuge in material things will never lead to deep joy or erase a feeling of loneliness. Nor will it contribute to a greater awareness of who you really are. It merely offers a temporary way out as something to hold on to, and that is the 'false' ego. I discussed this in chapter nine.

To know who you are, you need to be in touch with your heart and able to feel. Self-knowledge from the heart is about our inner depth. Our mind covers the surface, and that is also relevant in life. This could be described as the outer knowledge that serves us. While the language of our heart is the inner knowledge. In my practice, I regularly hear people say that they find it very difficult to properly hear the language of their heart. They then ask: 'How can I get more in touch with my feelings?' A question asked by both men and women who experience their thinking power drowning out the music like a powerful bass.

The good news is that someone who is asking themselves how to get better in touch with their feelings is aware that they have strayed and recognizes that they no longer want it to be that way. Therein lies the opening to change.

It is only once you know who you are and how you got to this point in your life, that you can give significance to the question: 'What do you really want?' At least in a meaningful way as rooted in the core of your 'being'. By increasing your self-awareness, you develop the ability to discover what suits you and what does not. The more powerful this image is for you, the more courage and readiness for action you will feel from within. This is by no means about your ego, or selfishness or self-centeredness.

"People enjoy exploring Tutankhamun's tomb in Egypt to discover mysteries, but overlook the mystery hidden in their own hearts." – Inayat Kahn

Your body language

Your body can play an important role in getting closer to your feelings. Your body knows better than anyone how you are doing, there is no escaping it. We have different forms of intelligence and tend to sometimes overlook our physical intelligence. Your spirit's health is an important measure of true health. The more aware you become of your physical state, the more it says about your state of awareness.

"Your physical body reveals your feelings and thoughts; your body is a miraculous temple of spirit."
– Barbara Hand Clow

Our emotional body communicates with us via our physical body and vice versa. I can still remember that at times of intense heartache, I literally could not eat, my body was busy 'digesting' other things. It is amazing how the mind and body work together, everything is interrelated and an ingenious set of connections. The well-intentioned advice to eat well did not help me at the time because that was just not the intention. I simply could not ignore what my body was telling me. Furthermore, I felt a deep trust that my body would automatically let me know when it had room again, even if it took weeks. That is what I did, I surrendered and trusted that this was the intention. And so, after a while, the appetite returned of its own accord.

> **Weak Spot**
> A short exercise to become aware of your body's physical signals.
> 1. What do you consider a 'weak spot' in your body?
> 2. Can you feel what it is connected to?
> 3. To what extent can you perceive its underlying message? And what is that message?

The better you learn to listen to yourself and pay attention to increasing your inner awareness, the more sensitive your physical system becomes. Many people have problems with sleeping for example, like Lisa.

Lisa told me she sometimes sleeps badly. She knows that her sleeping behavior is an expression of what is going on in her life. She went through an extreme period a while back: 'For months I slept a maximum of four hours a night. I have no idea how I kept going.' Each time she woke up, her thoughts ran away with her and there was no chance of getting back to sleep. She was in the midst of a move after a nasty divorce that was still fresh in her life. There was no point in resisting, she knew it was temporary. She had to get through this, and the best thing was to pay attention to everything that had to be done and, above all, to her own processing.

I am not a medical professional and by no means do I have all the answers, but I do know that a significant proportion of our complaints are psychosomatic and are trying to tell us something. How many people walk around with migraines, persistent pain, and other complaints? Many people push on against their better judgment when they are tired, because a deadline has to be met, or a project is demanding a lot. Your body does not lie, it is as simple as that.

I suffered myself in the past from severe pain in my lower abdomen for many years. At times I literally could not walk straight. I put up with this for a long time. I worked full-time, had a young family and time for myself was scarce. The physical pain was latent, unpleasant, and sometimes downright unbearable, limiting me in my activities. I eventually entered both the medical and the naturopathic scene, but the complaints remained. This continued until I quit my full-time interim work and started working with my coaching company and could create my own natural rhythm. I was the one who set my schedule and that is how I discovered that I need a lot of rest, space, and regularity in order to be well balanced physically. My symptoms disappeared in no time at all.

Your body will keep nagging at you until you get the message. Being yourself and getting to know yourself means taking your body as a vehicle seriously and honoring it. This is the body we have in this life, and it deserves taking good care of. How well do you know your body? To what extent can you deduce from your physical condition how you are doing?

You can work to increase the sensitivity of your body and thus your awareness. The more self-aware you become, the more sensitive you are to what your body does and does not accept. What you can pay attention to, for example, is:

- Being alert to how your body reacts to different foods
- Taking the time to eat and drink; not doing something else with a plate on your lap
- Paying attention to what you eat and enjoying it consciously
- Taking a break if you notice that you lack concentration or are tired
- Knowing what your ideal sleep rhythm is and acting accordingly
- Exercising and being attentive while indicating your limits.
- Listening to physical complaints, however subtle they may be, and doing something about them.
- Paying attention to your gut feeling. This is a physical sensation, for example an indefinable feeling that arises and cannot be explained immediately.

These points are not exhaustive, but a suggestion to train yourself to pay more attention to your body and your consciousness. Body and mind are like yin and yang. By this I mean less the contrast, than the interplay. The better you take care of your body, the better it is for your mental well-being, and also the better for being yourself. And vice versa, the better you take care of your inner well-being, the more your body benefits.

Independent, Yet Connected

Being who you are requires you to look at yourself with gentleness. You do not have to be perfect, in fact: it is precisely the rough edge we all possess that makes you unique and beautiful, exactly as intended. Daring to be completely yourself, looking at yourself with love and compassion, that means accepting that you are who you are, that you look the way you look, that you sound the way you sound, that you acknowledge your gift and take it into the world with love.

Many people suffer from attributing value to the approval of others. It can be approval from your partner, a manager, director, father, mother, or your child. The real foundation for being who you are is discovering that you can give yourself what you need, and that is not the approval of others. While writing this, I am aware of how difficult this is for some. Maybe you are a little sceptical because you have not yet discovered the true value of that statement. The more you are yourself, the more you love yourself and can be relaxedly yourself in trust, the better you will be able to free yourself from the idea that you need the approval of others.

We bare what lies inside us in our interaction with others, especially with loved ones. The connection helps you to get to know yourself even better. You are challenged to stay in your own center, on the dot in the circle. When you do that in a loving and respectful way, it creates a wonderful basis for self-expression and being relentlessly yourself. We do not need others to feel good at our foundation, at least not in a dependent sort of way.

Being independent and yet connected to others means

remaining yourself in a cooperation, friendship, or relationship. In my experience you enter the danger zone when you feel that you need the other person to complete the puzzle. It is possible to stay true to yourself in a cooperation, friendship, or love affair, when you move with each other – together and alone – but always in connection with each other, like a meandering river. That also means finding a natural balance between giving and being able to receive. It means taking responsibility for creating enough space for yourself, creating the conditions to remain close to your true you. From there, you can take up your space in the 'together' in a balanced way and also offer the other his space. You cannot expect your partner or business partner to take care of you, you can do that yourself. Just like you are not responsible for the other person. That is where it goes wrong, when we take on a false responsibility or place it on the other person.

Once you can see yourself as who you really are, it still takes courage to express this, by standing up for your value and taking space. More about this in chapter sixteen.

- ∞ Sometimes you need to change in order to remain yourself.
- ∞ Many women in the midlife phase search for the best way to combine their femininity with vigor and setting limits.
- ∞ Most men in the midlife phase discover that real meaning is found in living in contact with themselves and with others.
- ∞ Our emotional body communicates with us via our physical body and vice versa.

PART 4

DEEPEN YOUR GROWTH

13

MAKING HEARTFELT CHOICES

"The mind knows no answers. The heart knows no questions." – **Boeddha**

It was a long time ago, but that moment is still etched in my memory. I went to buy a present for a friend and was wandering around a large garden and home shop. What should I get her? There was so much choice! An hour and a half later, I was outside again, empty-handed. I felt lost. Not choosing seemed the best option as it leaves the door open for other, possibly better, options. The supposed freedom we think we are allowing ourselves by doing so, is in fact nothing more or less than postponement. In this chapter, I will be talking about how to make heartfelt choices to take you even closer to who you are. In doing so, I will be looking, amongst other things, at your core values and deepest desires.

From the moment we get out of bed, we make choices all day long, often without even realizing it. We decide whether to go running first or not, what we are going to wear and what to eat for breakfast. Many of the choices we make are done on automatic pilot. When walking on a beautiful path through the woods with sturdy roots emerging from the ground, we decide in a split second where to set the next foot. What about the choices we make for a new sofa, a new job, a new business concept or a partnership?

It is only when we take decisions that we create movement and discover the impact of our choice. When choosing, it is essential that you know yourself well. Each person has their own natural way of making decisions, which is best suited to them. There is therefore no one way, it also depends on how we are put together. Hence the importance of knowing how you can come to decisions in a way that suits your nature. I for example know not to take my bigger decisions in the moment, but to wait until my inner authority, which is driven by my emotions, shows me the way of its own accord. When I start forcing things, it comes from the mental side and that clouds my decision-making process. It brings a lot of peace to know what your natural way of making decisions is. You don't have to let anyone push you around, just follow the way that suits your nature.

Your core values help in clarifying who you are as a person and what you stand for. These values describe the core of your 'being', your identity. In this way your core values are not about what you are good at, such as your passions and talents. My core values for example are love, purity, connection, depth, and playfulness. These words represent in essence my state of being when I am purely myself and where I feel in a natural way, at my best. Whether in a business or personal context, it stays the same. I am relentlessly myself when this is in balance. By being aware of this, I know when I am centered at the core of my being and when I am not. For me, knowing this is of incredible value, it contributes to my quality of life, and serves, among other things, as a guide in the choices I make.

> **Your Core Values**
> Which core values best represent your identity? This should usually come to four or five, no more. This will make you focus and at the same time feel complete.
> If you find it difficult to formulate your core values, ask people around you who know you well for help and ask them how they see you as a person.

Knowing Your Deepest Desires

Knowing your deepest desires is a gateway for discovering what you really want and therefore very helpful in making heartfelt choices. This is not a need of the ego, but comes from the heart and soul.

To find out what it is you really desire, take a moment to consider the difference between your head (your thoughts) and your heart. The voice of your heart is often a mere whisper and is always constructive and solution oriented. Your heart will never speak in terms of 'should you be doing that' or 'you are not good enough'. Remembering that will already take you a long way. Whereas our ego, driven by our intellect, is very quick to ask, 'How are you going to do that?' or to worry about when it will happen.

Many people are so used to covering the voice of their heart with shouting their thoughts that they think there is no heart voice. Which of course is not the case, but you may need to work on it to be able to see or feel it (again). This requires acuity and for that you need to slow down, take a step back, find the silence within and listen. Remember that your heart is not shouting at you, so find peace and quiet in order to hear your heart's voice.

Hereafter is a writing exercise to help you clarify your deeper desires, also known as your soul's desires. These desires will then be reflected in your personal manifesto in chapter nineteen.

Deepest Desires
You can figure out your desires from different angles, such as your work, your social life or love relationship. This exercise helps you to feel your way through the process, to focus your energy on it, to trust it and radiate it out. From there, to believe and expect that sooner or later your desires will become reality in whichever capacity that may be. Make sure you call upon your desire from your heart. Take time therefore to find a nice place where you can write undisturbed. You can use the download at www.evelienvanes.com/download for this exercise.

Step 1 - Determine your approach
Decide where you want to figure out your desires, for example, in your job or in love. Make sure you disconnect from the current situation: your job, your company, or your current partner in love. In this way you avoid starting off with limitations. The idea is to begin with a clean canvas and to assume that everything is possible.

Step 2 - Visualization
Visualize and see yourself experiencing your desire. Close your eyes and use all your senses to experience what you are feeling as you experience it. What do you see, who are you with, what do you smell, what do you taste, what sensations do you feel in your body and how do you react

to these? Take your time, remain in the moment and bring your deepest desires to life in a visual way.

Step 3 - Writing
After your visualization, open your eyes and start writing. Formulate your sentences from how you feel, as if you were experiencing it in the moment, and then dig deeper. For example, 'I feel appreciated.' This does not say much on how you feel. Therefore, for everything you write down, ask yourself the why question. Repeat this question several times, until you get to the core from within and cannot answer a 'why' question any more. In this way you go one layer deeper and put the underlying feeling into words.

This exercise makes you step into the moment in all vividness, as if the desire were already there. In this way you awaken feelings and release energy that helps you create and manifest. This is how the natural law of attraction works on desire.

"You are what your deep, driving desire is. As your desire is, so is your will. As your will is, so is your deed. As your deed is, so is your destiny."
– Brihadaranyaka Unpanishad

Making Conscious Decisions

Having a clear understanding of your deeper desires creates an important foundation for making heartfelt choices. These choices are made because we count on them to bring us further in a positive sense and to contribute to our happiness in life. This is based on what we know, and think is right at that moment. 'Mistakes' in life are there to help us make different choices in future situations. To go in directions that feel right, that are heartfelt. It is often the painful choices we have made that ultimately teach us the most.

The fear of the unknown can have a paralyzing effect when making choices, but the closer you stay to your feelings, the less this effect is. This paralysis is mainly due to your fear being fed by your intellect, whereas when your heart is the motor, what you feel is purely healthy tension. What then prevails is the feeling of trust from following the call of your heart, which is so pure and deeply anchored that you feel you have nothing to fear if you follow it. Then, what is needed is the courage to go for your choice. When the impetus comes from your deepest roots, the chances are big you will take the step. You then move from a place of confidence that this is the right thing.

There are also people who are afraid of missing out in life, and postpone choices thinking there might be a better option ahead. Not choosing is losing. Take the leap, follow your heart, and discover how you can make new choices and start with a clean canvas at any time of the day. A pristine canvas that you can color in your own way and in your own time. Whether this means that you are without a job, without customers, without a love affair or without an owned property, so be it. These are all situations that you can experience as an opportunity and resource to make a new beginning. Every end, after all, is a new beginning. Embrace it and surrender to the space that is created and discover how this can be a great gift. It all depends on how you perceive things, there are so many possibilities from a place of freedom and space, to organize life's journey of discovery just the way you want it. Everything is possible.

It may be that during your decision process others come to you – solicited or unsolicited – with mostly kind and well-intentioned advice. Others have their own image of reality which they project onto you, which does not always make it easier to make your own choice. I have been told: 'Maybe it would be good for you to create some security now.' Whether in work or relationship situations, it has been said a few times in both contexts. I know that when I follow my heart, I can make choices that may not be obvious to others. I can be surprising and unpredictable, especially in the eyes of those more focused on certainty. In other words, stay close to your true self, to your feelings and trust them. They are the best adviser when it comes to heartfelt choices.

Living from your heart means disconnecting from the assault of information and the impulses of the outside world. Access inner silence so you can hear the voice of your soul. Your thoughts strongly determine how you feel and can lead you astray. Just as you can send your thoughts off course by tuning into another energy, thus changing them.

"Your heart will answer before you even finish the question." – Gregg Braden

Be careful when making choices to do not overanalyze things, as psychologist Gert Gigerenzer says: 'To make good decisions in a complex world, you have to be skilled at ignoring information.' In brief, be critical of the information you ingest to arrive at your choice and at some point, make a decision. Better a bad decision than no decision at all. The more exciting the choice and the greater its importance, the higher the risk that we get stuck in our thinking.

Making a choice implies that you are aware of the consequences that derive from it. I am not saying that impulse decisions are by definition wrong. But from experience I would say that conscious choices ensure that you can see the impact it will have in two respects:

1. Awareness of how the choice feeds you.
2. Realization of the effect your choice will have on the people who are affected by your decision, especially the people you love.

Consequences

Choices come with consequences and these consequences involve karma. Karma is a fundamental law that affects us all, whether we believe in it or not. We are all expected to live a pure life, staying true to ourselves, acting with integrity, and with compassion and respect for others, from the source of our inner love. We are given room to correct our own mistakes and to forgive others. By not doing so, we hinder in particular our own growth and development.

In Buddhism it is said, 'A man is born to the world he has made.' Based on my experience this statement essentially reflects the infinity of our soul which creates in earthly life a system of action and reaction. This occurs in this life, but also beyond. Our future is determined by the actions we take and the impact they have. Decisions are therefore crucial as they will either bring you closer to your soul, or further away from it.

When you make a choice and are still preoccupied with other options, in fact it implies you have not yet chosen. Your attention is indeed not on the choice you made. When you focus on the choice you made and it doesn't turn out as you had wanted, you can still today make another choice. Keep feeling and adjusting if that is what your heart is telling you.

The results of your actions can sometimes lead unintentionally to unwanted effects. Maybe a choice you made has a totally unexpected negative effect on you or the people around you. So long as your intention is pure, there is no reason to worry.

Sometimes in life there are certain lessons we need to learn; we then make choices that lead us via a diversion. Like a big loop on our path to our soul's destination. Many will not even be aware of this, and that is fine. There is no soul here that incarnates and walks in a straight line to its final destination. Everyone needs to develop in some way or another, that is the essence of our existence in this life.

Every being is confronted at some time with choices they wish they had made differently. This provides us with valuable lessons that enrich our lives. You could see your missteps as signposts. Time will tell whether the choice you made turns out to be the right one and contributes to more joy in your life. Make time to feel the impact of your choice, this requires you to focus on the choice you have made. We each get a chance to start again in life, no matter our baggage, and not just once but many times, as long as we take responsibility for what we do and what we decide to do.

Being aware of the thought alone that we have a choice in every situation, already allows us to feel more positive about the circumstances. I will help you below, with the guidance of some concrete questions, to become even more aware of how you make choices.

> **Making Conscious Choices**
>
> **1. Recognizing patterns**
> Figure out how you usually arrive at your choices. Look back at the major most impactful decisions you have made so far, but also at the less significant choices. Think of a few concrete examples and go back to how you dealt with the different choices. How much time did you take and what was the process leading up to your choice?
>
> **2. Knowing your core values and desires**
> What are your core values and desires? Knowing yourself is an indispensable basis for making conscious and heartfelt choices. Your core values and desires are helpful here. Your core values express what you are like as a person and what you stand for; they are guiding principles for behavior and a guide for decision making. In addition to your core values as part of your personal signature, or inner compass, your deepest desires also play an important part. Knowing from deep within your heart how you want to feel is the most powerful form of clarity you can create.
>
> **3. Distinguishing between heart and head**
> Were the important choices you have made so far in your life heartfelt or did you make them from your thought-power? Do you find it difficult to distinguish between the two?

We tend to make things more complicated than they really are. Stand still for a moment, or sit or lie down in a comfortable spot, and place your hand on your heart, close your eyes and feel the physical beat of your heart. Stay centered, make contact with your heart. You will find answers in the silence. The answer is there, the question is only whether you will submit to it. You will lose the answer if you rush into your thoughts. Telling someone else what is going on inside of you can also help. Mirroring creates clarity.

4. **Knowing the impact of your choices**
To what extent do you take the consequences of your decisions into account; for yourself and the people affected by the decision? Take one of your examples and note to what extent you were aware of the consequences of your choice beforehand and what those consequences were.

5. **Choosing in autonomy**
How do the opinions of others affect the choices you make? Sharing and expressing yourself to others who can listen to you without judgment is valuable, but be careful not to take other people's opinions for the truth. There is no single truth, only what you experience. Others often react from their frame of reference and their image of reality and that has nothing to do with you. The more powerfully you stand in your own center, the more clearly you can make this distinction.

6. **Knowing your own pace**
At which pace do you make decisions? It is important to make decisions at the pace that suits you. For most people, it is advisable to sleep a night on important decisions, and

> even several nights on major, impactful decisions. This has everything to do with taking the time to consider the consequences of one's choices.

You cannot make wrong decisions if they are based on your heart. They can only lead to life lessons, lessons that always bring value, even though you may not (yet) see it in the moment.

- ∞ Know the best way for you to come to heartfelt choices.
- ∞ The voice of your heart is often a whisper and it is always constructive and solution oriented.
- ∞ Knowing your deepest desires is a gateway to discovering what you really want.
- ∞ When you make a choice, do it with conviction.
- ∞ Making a decision while still considering other options, means that you in fact have not yet made a choice.
- ∞ You become aware of how you make your choices, by:
  - Recognizing patterns
  - Knowing your core values and desires
  - Distinguishing between heart and head
  - Knowing the impact of your choices
  - Choosing in autonomy
  - Knowing your own pace

14

CREATE LOVING RELATIONSHIPS

"Love is the greatest force in the universe, and the source of our personal love energy lies in our hearts. The goal is that eventually we become love again, as love is our eternal nature." **– Christina von Dreien**

Love is not an impulse, but a deep-lying feeling that flows from a source of inner wisdom. I shared in chapter eight, how self-acceptance and self-love are at the base of self-esteem, the same can be said for love. Love goes a step further than that and is an essential foundation of everything we do in our lives, our work being no exception. I will look into how you learn about yourself through the other, into the different levels within love relationships that bring you even closer to yourself. I also discuss the difference between promises and intentions and how you can benefit from this in all aspects of your life. I further examine love as a basis in working relationships.

Learning via the Other

You learn the most about yourself through all kinds of connections and relationships. That is the way after all to be mirrored and confronted. You discover who you are through the deeper connection with the other person, you see when your ego, your thoughts and emotions are getting the better of you. Suppose you repeatedly fall for partners who are insensitive or who you feel you need to save. This is a signal for you to take a look at what is going on at a deeper level within you, causing you to do so. Ingrained patterns and values that we have taken on and that we believe are part of our DNA, are at the root of why we do what we do, even though they do not bring us the joy that we really want.

We all know someone in our environment who has been with the same life partner from a young age, or maybe this even applies to you. I cannot help but look with wonder and also admiration, at how you can stay connected through all life phases and personal transformations. Without making major concessions to your own development and life journey for the sake of the other. Each person is different and there is no one way to live life. There are people who can continue to develop themselves within the setting of a lifelong relationship with a partner. There are others who need different partners to come closer to themselves and discover who they truly are.

I used to sometimes claim. 'I'm not very good with men.' Now I laugh about it. The men in my life were my mirrors, enabling me to feel my own roots and learn to be myself. After all, you have to know yourself well in order to be able to attract a partner who feeds your soul and with whom you feel there is space for you to remain true to yourself. That is being who you are.

Your romantic partner and your friends are important,

but they are by no means the bedrock of your life happiness. This does not take away from how wonderful it is to have good friends and a warm, loving, and equal relationship. Many people however are trapped in a connection which is not right for them or are afraid of being alone and make themselves dependent on a partner. In doing so, they continually put the brakes on their personal expansion.

I regularly see this in practice in the business context too. Business partners who are attached to their company and hold on to the comfort and security of the connection. There often comes a point of irritation when the so-called safety and comfort are no longer valid. This is when a reassessment of individual dreams, desires and paths of development is needed to ensure that neither business partner disappears in the collective.

Love Relationships on Different Levels

You can experience a love relationship on a number of different levels, namely:
1. Spiritual
2. Physical
3. Emotional
4. Mental

In a heart born relationship, the basis of the attraction is spiritual. This is a feeling of connection with someone at the level of the soul, whereby the roots of the love go deeper than merely to personality level or that of physical attraction.

A merely physical and emotional connection with a partner can make your head spin. You then focus on safety and wanting to do everything together, while in fact you are creating a false sense of security. When you are not aware of what is happening and feel head over heels in love, you can convince yourself that the picture is perfect. Appearances are deceptive and there is a good chance that the picture will prove to be extremely fragile in the long run when you discover that the connection at soul level is missing.

The mental stratum is about being able to *level* with someone on an intellectual plane, to be able to spar and exchange ideas. Humor, too, is an expression of the mental level and can have a connecting effect.

The love for a partner with whom you initially feel a spiritual connection is deeper and more enduring than when this is not the case. 'You can be touched at soul level by the spirit of another in a way that intensely enriches you and connects you with your source without losing your own individuality,' says Kribbe. In a spiritual relationship, you do not fuse with each other.

Quite extraordinary here is that a soul connection can be established in a very short period of time. A spiritual relationship such as this brings peace, deep trust and a quiet knowing that this is how it is meant to be. You see each other for who you are and give each other the space to be. You respectively share without fear of consequences. Time is irrelevant in a spiritual relationship. It is being relentlessly yourself, staying close to your core and feeling a deep love for someone for who they are. In such a relationship the other person is in fact not much more than a trigger to let the love – which is already within you – flow. It also means, as Jan Geurtz aptly says: 'A relationship in which you recognize that the relationship is not more important than you are.' Be alert to this false loyalty or you risk becoming alienated from yourself and then, one day you will inevitably meet yourself.

So, how do you recognize a love at soul level? If you are asking yourself that question, the chances are you have not yet come across one. You know when it happens, you can feel how special the connection is and how much deeper it goes. Just remember that eyes are the gateway to the soul. What do you see and feel when you look deeply into each other's eyes?

There is a difference between letting go and losing a love that was on a physical and emotional level and the end of a spiritual connection. When you have a spiritual connection with someone, you will find that you always carry the connection with this soul with you in a certain way, even once the love affair is over. This does not have to burden you in the long run. A love at soul level certainly needs time to heal, needs you to learn from it and gain insights about yourself and how this partner helped you in your development. So that you can cherish the love that was there.

Recovering from a love that was on a personality level differs yet again. It may feel terribly painful and intense, but you get through it quicker seen it was founded on quicksand. That person will remain in your memory, but not with the intensity and depth with which a soul connection remains part of your life.

"Despite how open, peaceful, and loving you attempt to be, people can only meet you as deeply as they've met themselves." – *Matt Kahn*

Promises and Intentions

It is important to clear out and purify to avoid carrying negative baggage with you. On the one hand, emotional luggage that can hinder your development, and on the other, negative baggage that can burden others who have nothing to do with it nor can do anything with it. Whether this is a business partnership, a marriage, living together or selling a house. Suppose you have sold the house where you lived with great pleasure. Then close this phase off in a way worthy of it, detach yourself in order to be able to look back at it with gratitude. When you do that, you give yourself the chance of happiness in a new place. Create a ritual that works for you, this opens your heart to new experiences.

If you are in a relationship with someone and have felt for a long time that it would be better for each other's development to let go and each walk a different path, then it cannot be the intention that past promises hold you back. How many people, based on a promise, a pledge of allegiance, or feelings of guilt towards children or partner, remain within the status quo even though they know deep down inside that this is wrong? Life is about remembering who you are and living from that precept. That does not mean denying yourself or others. Pledging your allegiance to someone else can never take priority over your own soul's development. Should you do so, you will then discover sooner or later that the diversions you chose to take, bring you back to where you were.

There is a big difference between promises and intentions. Intentions are powerful and create space, whereas promises tend to lock you in, rather than allow you room to be who you are and develop from there. I would like to focus on an example, marriage, which is by definition an institution in which promises are made and recorded. I myself have never been married but did dream for a certain period of the romantic picture. That longing was essentially about experiencing an equal, deepening, and loving relationship with a self-aware partner.

In life, you must above all remain true to your own journey of development and never sacrifice your soul's evolution for someone else.

To quote Christina von Dreien, when we die 'we may leave our physical bodies behind, but we take our patterns of thought, belief, feeling and behavior with us, in the form of energetic information, to our next incarnations. Promises, vows, and oaths are particularly problematic, as they are often accompanied by the words "forever" or "never" or "for eternity". It is quite possible that certain beliefs, or belief systems, promises, vows and the like, are no longer relevant in a later life, because in the meantime, the soul has developed further in a certain area. But as long as these things are not cleared away, they form a blockade and an obstacle to the soul's future development.' This resonated with me when I read it and I can feel how it applies to many forms of promises.

Love as a Foundation

It is only when you feel self-love and can remove negative and loaded feelings towards yourself, that you can love others. That is inner wisdom. Understanding how important it is to love yourself is one thing, actually acting on it by being kind to yourself and loving yourself is another.

Love is all-embracing and is not only about self-love or love for those close to you that you hold dear. It is looking with compassion and a soft heart at everything that lives, at the Earth and all that moves on it, with respect for nature. It is the seemingly small things that make the difference, but which are large in terms of energy. The smile on a stranger's face in the street and a kind word to someone who holds his super-enthusiastic dog on a leash for you while you are running. It is paying someone an unexpected and heartfelt compliment, but also overcoming your fear and catching a spider and bringing it outside. It sounds a bit ridiculous, but do not be mistaken; therein lies the power of love for all living things. It affects your feelings and energy.

Love is the foundation of the work you do, as long as it is done from a pure heart, with compassion and feeling for your clients, contacts, and the people you work with. In my work, I feel involved with my clients and can look at them with love. That is the breeding ground for them to achieve great results.

It is only once you are connected to the core of love from your soul that you can feel relaxation and experience that you are 'whole'. That means feeling that things are good the way they are, feeling trust and inner peace and that you are the one creating the conditions for life the way you want to live it.

For me, feeling love is at the foundation of my being. Remembering who I am, where I come from and what my source is. This may sound elusive to you. The words you use are not important, it is about what you feel around it, what it does to you and how you can deepen the love you sense and experience. The more you know what you need and what you can give yourself, the better you are able to stay in 'loving being'. Personally, that means taking a lot of time for myself to connect with my inner source, to enjoy the open air, the sun and the sea and to ground myself. In this way I can really be who I am, feel trust and take my place in my work, in friendships, in love, in everything.

It is only later on that I found my way to further integrate my intuition into my (working) life from who I am at the core. In this, the cognitive, intuitive, and spiritual coincide beautifully. My basic education was mainly cognitive. However, by nature I have the need to make contact on a deeper level, so that I can connect from there with others and with myself. Only then can a meaningful connection be made.

I evaluate my life based on the extent to which I feel love flow. If I notice that I am in danger of going off the rails, because for example I am affected by something or someone, I then know what I need to return to myself. I am aware that I must make this a priority, even if it means adapting my agenda. I feel what is needed to restore the balance within me. I know, as I am quite sensitive, that if a situation arises in which I need to make a reset, I can do it in a short space of time. Which does not mean that my thoughts don't get the best of me every now and then and that I take a fall. That is life and that is what makes us human. But for me, life is no longer lived in the fast lane. I know what serves me and what does not, the only thing I can do is stand up for it and express it.

The next exercise is to become aware of the extent to which you allow yourself to be driven by love in everything you do. This may seem easy to answer but take the time to observe yourself and be completely honest with yourself. This is how you will best be of service to yourself.

> **Approaching with Love**
> 1. What is your perception of how you usually approach everything and everyone around you? It is in the little things.
> 2. Test your self-image with others by asking how they see you approach others.
> 3. How do you approach clients, contacts and cooperation partners? And how do you approach people in a private context?
> 4. What would you like to do differently in terms of how you approach people and situations?
> 5. What do you need in order to start doing this today?

Maintain a Sense of Wonder

Every healthy relationship, including a cooperation, consists of a fine balance between unity and individuality. I also call it together and alone, connection and autonomy. That is, experiencing what 'together' brings, in the form of deepening, development and joy, the effect of one plus one is eleven. And in addition, time for yourself to walk your own path and fulfil your soul's mission. Whatever that may be. That means making sure you are in balance inside.

Suppose you have a business partner who always starts work early, whereas you are not a morning person. How do you deal with that? Do you force yourself to be at work before dawn every day? Or do you reframe this in a way that works for both of you? Be creative, there are many options out there without doing yourself violence.

Breathing space and some distance go a long way in potentially keeping a relationship vibrant. That means not only doing things together, but also partly maintaining your own life, with your own friends and your own work. How wonderful it is to be there for each other, but sometimes also choose for your own space which nourishes your spirit. This keeps your relationship healthy and exciting, so long as you share enough special moments and adventures together. Kribbe says it is about 'the female tendency towards transcendence and unity', while individuality stands for 'the male tendency towards freedom and individuality. Both poles are necessary for a spirited game of connectedness and individuality, a wonderful mix of safety and adventure.'

Real love is about being whole and at one with yourself, that is the starting point for any healthy relationship. Your romantic partner is in fact your mirror to love loving yourself even more. The better you know yourself and can access the core of who you are, the more wonderful your relationships will be.

"The source of love is pure consciousness. The key to genuine love is accessing the expanded awareness of our true self." – Deepak Chopra

A certain familiarity develops in each relationship after a while, which is not something to fear or see as the beginning of the end. A certain familiarity can also be pleasant. What is important is that you maintain a sense of wonder in relation to each other. That you never, ever take each other for granted. Maintaining your autonomy in a relationship prevents the 'love' from suffocating. *You* create a way for the love to flow and that is the golden key in every relationship.

- ∞ Love in any form is staying true to yourself and not denying others the same right either, if you feel that the connection does not serve both of your individual development paths.
- ∞ Remaining true to your own path of development means never placing your soul's evolution after that of another.
- ∞ Love is all-embracing. It is looking with compassion and a soft heart at yourself and everything that lives, the Earth and all that moves on it with respect for nature.
- ∞ Love is a deeper feeling that comes from a source of inner wisdom.
- ∞ The better you know yourself and can get to the core of who you are, the more wonderful your relationships in life will be.

15

GAIN ENERGY THROUGH DREAMING

"It is the possibility of having a dream come true that keeps life interesting." – **Paulo Coelho**

Seeing our dreams fulfilled is glorious and extraordinary, yet the challenge lies in the fact that we are always creating new dreams in our lives. Having dreams is powerful in that it gives us life energy and is good for our mental state. This, therefore, is an indispensable chapter to reflect on if you want to be even more yourself, and if you want to position yourself from what you have to offer. It is also important in the run-up to drawing up your own manifesto at the end of chapter nineteen. I will guide you, among other things, through doing that which brings you satisfaction and concretizing your dreams, so that your energy is fed in a positive sense. I will also be discussing the role of certainty in your life and help you become aware of your moments of bliss.

It is great to be fulfilled and have a sense of purpose in the work we do, but the status quo in itself is not the spice of life. The big picture is what we are talking about here and dreams are an indispensable part of it. By dreams I mean the yearning for experiences from our pure source of 'being', so not the wishes for materialistic things.

The zeitgeist we are currently living in means that people's pursuit to be constantly experiencing maximum satisfaction through their jobs, may have gone a bit too far. Work is there as a means to make a living and if you can do that in a way that brings you fulfilment, that is fantastic. Life is about feeling good, being able to be who you are and experiencing fulfilment and meaning in your life, one way or the other. It is quite conceivable that you have found a way of experiencing satisfaction through your work, but maybe not fully and add to it via a hobby, voluntary work or in some other way. You instinctively know when it is right for you or not and when you want and can change things. In life, you are responsible only to yourself and to no one else.

Back to your dreams. What do you dream of and do you allow yourself to (day) dream at all? Most of us take little time to stop and reflect on our dreams. And yet the power and energy they release is blissful. In order to make dreams more concrete, it can help to visualize them, write, draw, or paint them, or discuss them with someone you can easily talk to. Speaking out is a powerful way of making your dreams come alive. Release them and throw them into the universe. The clearer you are on what you want to create, the stronger you will attract them. The following exercise will help you with this.

> **Visualizing Your Dreams**
>
> I will, based on a number of questions, help you to consciously consider how you want to integrate dreams into your life.

1. What do you dream of?
2. When do you daydream, where are you, and how does this come about?
3. What dreams do you have about your company in particular, or about your career? What does that look like, what are you doing and who are you with?
4. Which way do you use to specify your dreams so you can turn them into intentions? Think of the form that suits you best.
5. Then visualize your dreams. You can then also choose something – a kind of anchor – that symbolizes your dream.
6. Would you like to plan the frequency in which you reflect on your dreams? A big stick comes in handy to make sure you make the time. You can make it a ritual, per month, quarter, or year. The trick is to feel what works for you and what you want to realize.
7. With whom would you like to discuss your dreams? And then take action and do it. Sharing helps you to make your dreams even more concrete.

It is valuable to do this as a one-off exercise, but if you follow up on it by doing it more regularly, it will have more impact.

The Importance of Security

A certain amount of security is important for most people, but it need not always be related to work. Some would not dare to leave their job without a new prospect, no matter how miserable they are or how much energy their current job costs them. Others, on the other hand, do not lose any sleep over it; they feel confident and know that they will manage somehow. They are able to enjoy the space that is created to explore new paths and feel the freedom to make new choices.

There are several factors that influence the degree to which a person aspires for certainty, namely:

1. Your nature and your design (see the boxed text below). There are people who, regardless of (financial) security, have an intrinsic drive to be independent. The degree of safety has hardly any influence on them.
2. Personal circumstances. Receiving an inheritance for example might bring you a sense of safety, making you more relaxed and carefree.
3. The stage of life you are in. The life phase for example which starts in your fifties usually brings more inner peace than the turbulent time around the age of thirty and later in midlife around the age of forty (see chapter twelve).

> **Human Design**
> The Human Design system combines astrology, the chakras, I Ching, the Kabbalah, quantum mechanics, biochemistry, and DNA genetics. Human Design functions from the principle that your possibilities and limitations are already determined the moment you are born. Your birth-imprint is shown with a Body Graph.

Satisfaction Does Not Come From 'Head' Issues

When do you feel satisfaction in your work and your life? Isn't it, like happiness, about the absence of striving for it? Precisely that, because the moment it becomes an issue for you, it means something is wrong.

One of the statements I regularly hear is: 'I want to maximize my potential.' It is an almost automatic statement to express a certain feeling of dissatisfaction with your work or life. While the question is: what are you doing about it? Do you actually know what your potential is, or as I would rather call it: what your unique added value is so that you can enlarge it? What I see is that many people are insufficiently clear on this. You could ask yourself why, if you do know your unique added value, you do not know how to find your way forward? It may have something to do with the patterns I mentioned earlier, which prevent you from moving forward and putting it to good use. Think, for example, of a lack of self-confidence, self-esteem, courage, taking up space, drive and determination to take action. Or the craving for certainty, which I mentioned earlier on. In my experience, when you know what your unique added value is, the fire that burns from within is extremely bright and powerful. To illustrate this, I'll share Emily's story.

Emily is a budding entrepreneur, in her late thirties, with a full-time job. She is trying to figure out what exactly she wants with her business. When she came to me, she explained how she wants to use her talents as project manager and planning and structuring expert to advise clients. A smart woman, committed to development and with an enormous drive to get her business off the ground. The hesitation she felt was around how to go about it, and between the lines I sensed that she was not yet fully convinced that this was the way for her.

We dived deep during the first coaching session and talked about her background, including her childhood and upbringing. While at first, I could sense her head's impatience to move forward, I took her by the hand into the depths and she shared her story. She told me how she had been working for years on her own childhood and adolescence traumas and how they had had a huge impact on her life, still did today. She shared how important it is for her to be engaged in her growth and development and how she seeks this in her work.

During the conversation, she realized that her original business idea was not the right one for her. It was like a bolt of lightning. Suddenly she could see herself from the outside, as an observer and realized that she had unilaterally constructed her business idea from her head. She felt very clearly that this would not bring her the fulfilment she longed for. She had constantly resisted the idea of doing 'heart things' in her work because she had come such a long way in this herself. This made her feel that it would be too much of a burden for her.

As we discussed this, I saw her take on the feeling that her own development and healing would be a valuable source of inspiration for others and that this would, moreover, help her further in her own growth, development, and healing. This is how Emily started to work as a mentor.

Emily's story stresses how fulfilment and meaning never come from 'head' issues, but from the heart and the soul. No matter how wonderful and promising your business idea may seem, if it is not grounded in your essence, it will not fulfil you.

Finally, a dimension that I would like to add is the contribution to a greater whole. Fulfilment is a feeling that could be described as ecstasy and it is harder to experience when it is purely for your own benefit. It is only when you do something that has meaning for something outside yourself, outside your personality, that you will experience a state of bliss. Bliss can be seen as a state of being that is joyful and enjoyable and brings a magical feeling. It is a wonderful sensation of excitement, a 'top of the world' feeling that is not continuous but in the moment. RJ, who organized the largest underwater clean-up operation in history with over six hundred professional divers from all over the world, is a great example of bliss. He explained how making this statement with so many other people, brought him a powerful sense of fulfilment and excitement.

It is valuable to be aware of when you experience your top of the world moments, which can be both business-related and personal.

> **Your Moments of Bliss**
> What moments of bliss have you experienced recently? Describe the situation and the sensations you felt.

Some people realize how scarce moments of bliss are in their lives. This can be confronting, but at the same time it is a start to make sure that you consciously create these moments in your life.

> *"Don't bring the light to the world, be the light. If you do so, everywhere you are, it feels brighter."*
> **– Abraham Hicks**

- ∞ Daydreaming contributes positively to our life energy and mental state of being.
- ∞ There are several factors that influence the degree to which a person desires safety:
    - Your nature, your design
    - Personal circumstances
    - Your stage of life
- ∞ A sense of fulfilment comes from the heart and soul and not from 'head' issues.

16

TAKING UP YOUR OWN SPACE

Having clear dreams, knowing who you are and what you want, are the starting point for owning your space. Taking up your own space through force of thought often overshoots the mark. Owning and occupying space is about being visible, about having courage, not hiding and not being afraid that you are doing things wrong. It is about occupying your place out of intentions that are pure. I will help you in this chapter, become aware of how you can own and occupy space.

Knowing you are going to fail and doing it anyway.
Taking the plunge with your eyes open, even though you are scared.
Resigning without having another job.
Ending a friendship because it no longer works and costs you energy rather than creating it.
Booking a trip alone, far away, without knowing exactly where you are going, just because you feel you are meant to.
Living on your own terms because your heart tells you to, and not going along with how it should be.
Engaging in a tense conversation with sweaty palms and expressing what can be said so you can remain true to yourself.

Suppose you walk in somewhere and there is someone at the entrance. Often enough that person will say 'sorry'; women in particular tend to say this automatically when they feel they are in the way. They shy away and apologize in advance for being where they are, for standing where they stand. People sometimes apologize for their very existence. Yes, you read correctly: for their very existence. For the fact of being somewhere.

'If you are not living on the edge, you are taking up too much space' is a quote by mountaineer Jim Whittaker that caught my eye and touched me. It is about taking on life, being brave and daring. Apologizing for your existence touches on a collective theme, that of the domination of male energy, and the subordination of women, in a way that has become pervasive and leaves its footprints in the world we live in. Have you ever heard a man say sorry in a situation like above?

'Sorry' is a word that some people use all the time, and which touches on the theme of taking up space. Just think about it: how often do you say 'sorry' and what for exactly? The more attention you pay to it, the more alert you will become to it in others.

Use the word 'sorry' sparingly and only when there is a real reason for a sincere apology, but not out of a habit which leads you to short-change yourself unnecessarily. Every person has an equal right to be there and to occupy, also literally, their space.

Occupying Space in Midlife

The theme of claiming our space is common to both men and women and recurs in various phases of life (see chapter twelve). I will take a closer look at the influence of the polarities that emerge in men and women during the midlife phase. Both genders are searching for a way to create room for their female sensitive side.

Women have literally learned to know their place and stick to it. We live in a society that has been driven by male energy for centuries. These times are changing, women are breaking free from the place they have traditionally taken, while retaining their feminine energy. For women, this is an individual journey of discovery that will contribute to the collective. It is about taking up space and speaking out from the male force within.

The midlife stage in particular, serves as a catalyst in this. For women, this is often a restless phase in which they discover how they can tap into their strength from the male energy dormant within them. What adds to the challenge is that nowadays many women have children somewhat later than nature intended. It is precisely in this phase of their lives that it is crucial to make time for themselves on a structural basis, in order to create clarity on who they really are, what they have to do and why. In such a way that they then occupy their space with authenticity and can make their contribution to the greater whole, without overcompensating from their male strength. For women, this is about speaking out and is linked to the throat; the throat chakra.

The impact of the current COVID-19 pandemic on the division of roles within the home is great. Many women have lapsed into a nurturing role, helping out with home-schooling children and struggling to claim their me-time in the family and take up their space. This role is deeply rooted and therefore it is unfortunate to witness this fall back. One example of this is the male-female ratio when it comes to visibility in the media. Where men are still clearly more visible, a slight improvement had been noticed in the past ten years though not yet at the level of a balanced distribution. The current zeitgeist is throwing a spanner in the works, with a decline in the male-female ratio in terms of visibility in the media. There is still a long way to go in this respect.

Men witness in their midlife phase an invitation to allow themselves to be gentler and milder so that they can learn to trust their intuition more and get out of their heads. A strive for freedom has developed for many men into a resistance to connection. There is a fear of opening up in the contact with another, and what started out as an urge for freedom degenerated into an ego that can no longer open up to anything but itself. Man's autonomy then leaves no room for the other, for a relationship based on equality.

More and more men are becoming aware of the impact of allowing their inner feminine energy and 'the midlife phase gives men the space to do so', says Clow. Men are rebalancing their feminine energy from their heart, the *heart chakra*, which makes them more complete. Both men and women basically have an intuitive radar. Many people are not aware of the subtle signs and promptings they receive. The very fact that it is said that women are much more intuitive, shows the kind of world we live in. Men and women have at the base, an intuitive radar.

Men need to be in live contact with themselves and others, that is where they find the true source of meaning. It is such a wonderful breath of fresh air to meet men who are self-aware and open to allowing that gentleness, while at the same time maintaining their masculinity. I feel blessed to have more and more men in my life who are discovering or have discovered this.

Women could do with some encouragement and support to take up their space in all purity, just as self-aware men could do to open their hearts.

Be Heard

I talked earlier about the importance for women of opening the *throat chakra* around the age of forty. I am sharing, in that context my story with you.

I have 'suffered' for years from regular throat clearing. A number of people in my immediate surroundings had even noticed it. It bothered me and I tried to get rid of it. That turned out to be more complicated than I thought. Not doing it was not an option, as I could feel that I really needed to clear my throat in order to produce a clear voice. I even ended up seeing an EAR, NOSE AND THROAT *doctor, which did not help. At some point I resigned myself and stopped paying attention to it.*

It was not until I started looking into what happens to men and women in midlife that I gained a wonderful insight. I read about women and taking up space and speaking out and realized in a moment of lucidity that I hadn't suffered from throat clearing for ages. Except for when I had a cold.

I see my throat clearing complaints as signals from my body, linked to the theme of taking up space, of speaking out. In retrospect, this is something I should have done much more of, especially in the years when I was suffering from it. It is only once I allowed myself to be relentlessly myself, to express more of what was going on inside of me, that the chronic symptoms disappeared like snow melts in the sun. When it does still rear its head, I know that there is something going on under the surface that makes me hold back from taking up space and speaking out.

How incredible that our bodies let us know where we need to pay attention. In her book *The Key to Self-liberation*, life philosopher, Christiane Beerlandt, has this to say about the psychological meaning of the throat, 'To be able to speak and stand up for yourself. Freeing yourself, on the one hand by being able to smoothly take in emotional experiences and on the other hand by expressing in a self-confident way what you consider necessary to communicate.'

I talked about taking up space with fellow entrepreneur, Susan, on a beautiful sunny day in a clearing in the woods. We sat on a tree trunk and mused about taking up space.

Me: What does taking up space mean to you?
Susan: Taking up space is actually having the courage to make your aura bigger.

Me: What exactly do you mean by that?
Susan: For me, expanding your aura means bringing the energy of who you are into the world a little bit more. Allowing other people to come in contact with it, without your sucking up the other person's energy and taking over. Occupying your own space is, in my experience, being so powerful that you dare to let your energy flow and dare make it a little bigger without fear of its effect.

Me: Making it bigger is not the same as exaggerating it. It is about just being there. Just like the tree in front of us, standing there, blossoming, it is there in its own individuality, with its branches spread wide.
Susan: Yes, that tree does not make its aura smaller for the tree next to it. It does not think: let me hold back. They stand next to each other. Trees take up their space and merge into each other in nature.

Me: And so it is with us people, there is enough space for us all to be there, to take up our space.

Talking of the space we have here on Earth, I am reminded of the book *The Little Prince*, where the main character marvels at how much space we have here on Earth. And so it is, there is no lack of space and there is no need to blow out of proportion. Taking up space is about taking up space with purity, but also without excessive modesty.

When you take up space by force, it is often not very effective. The action then comes from a one-sided hard masculine energy. Whereas showing courage from a place of trueness and in line with the feminine energy, is pure. Every human being has this potential, but not everyone shows it or has yet discovered the way to it. Outshouting yourself serves no one, least of all yourself. It only takes you further away from your own core and will create an indefinable and uneasy feeling. In fact, it fuels your insecurity. The courage you show from soft and flawless feminine energy, enables you to learn life's valuable lessons, lessons that make your inner wisdom grow.

You get to share what is going on inside of you, and thereby taking up space on all fronts of your life, by doing it frequently and discovering what it brings you. Further on in your personal manifesto, you will be able to state how you stand in life and how you take up your space.

Standing in the Middle of the Circle

Taking up space from a connection with your soul means you need to eventually stand at the middle of the circle, at your center. I shall highlight three aspects to get there. Taking up space:

1. Requires you to be aware of the patterns of self-sabotage that have become part of your system.
2. Requires you to accept and value yourself for who you are. This includes not worrying about making mistakes and feeling safe, with yourself, to be who you are and be visible to the world.
3. Means letting the judgments and opinions of others slip you by.

To start with the first point: remaining in your own center and being aware of the extent to which you sabotage yourself. By self-sabotage I mean creating obstacles for yourself and actually only making things more difficult for yourself. We all do so, often without being aware of it. Think of procrastinating, denying our true needs and the negative emotions our ego evokes, such as power, envy, and irritation. It is an illusion to think you can remove the triggers, accept that they will always be there and that this is part of life. Where you do have a choice, is in deciding how you deal with them, as you can teach yourself to react differently to triggers. Become aware of what is happening inside of you, how you react and what options you can envisage to change this.

Self-acceptance and self-esteem (see also chapter eight) are crucial conditions for taking up space. It is only once you fully accept yourself as you really are, with all your wonderful qualities as well as the flaws, that there will be room for you to truly value yourself. That is believing in yourself, loving yourself and hardening the skin on your soul to let go of the fear of 'not doing it right'. What is the worst that could happen if you don't say or do something right? Let go of the idea that it has to be perfect. By the way. For most people who cite perfection as a reason for not taking up space, it appears not to be a matter of perfection at all, but in fact the fear of showing themselves as they really are.

Self-esteem really has to come from your soul. Even if you are standing in front of a room of two hundred, five hundred or a thousand people who are hanging on your every word and think you are fantastic, that is not what it is about and it will not last. Value comes from feeling that you are touching and inspiring others with what you do, from your authentic source and unique roots.

I mentioned detaching yourself from the opinions, convictions, and judgments of others as a third aspect for occupying space. People are, after all, human beings and usually quick to form opinions. What others think and feel is often a reflection of their own inner world. Turn your attention inwards, to your own story, to yourself and let go of what is not yours. We all have a lot of work to do in this respect.

There is no space scarcity, and there never will be. There is a place and a stage available for every person acting from a pure heart, in connection with their soul and with compassion for others. Being more concerned with walking our own path and less concerned with what others think or do would be helpful. Live your own life, be kind to yourself, respect each other and cherish the people around you that you love. Let us move beyond labels and judgments and give each other room to occupy space.

Have you ever experienced expressing your mischievousness, anger, frustration or discontent and being told (or feeling) this was not allowed, not possible or inappropriate? A friend has told me a few times that what she loves the most are the moments I show my rough edges. Those are the moments when I take people by surprise by what I say or do, when I am mischievous or unpredictable and don't conform to what is customary or expected of me. That too is in line with who I am. It is so precious to have people around you who know how to awaken this in you and who encourage you to take up space from a pure heart.

> **Occupying Space**
> I have a few questions to help you become even more aware of the extent to which you let yourself be seen and occupy space:
> 1. Which aspects of your nature do you maybe not show enough, but which are an important part of who you are?
> 2. List all the beliefs, assumptions, and thoughts that you have and suppress in order to be relentlessly yourself.
> 3. Which people stand in your way and drain your energy causing you to not occupy enough space?

4. Name the people in your environment who encourage you to take the stage and express what is going on inside of you.
5. What else do you need to be able to show more of yourself as you really are?

Being aware of the extent to which you take up space and of the influence your environment has on this, enables yourself to make choices in this domain in such a way that you dare to take up your space.

In order to occupy space, it is important to be relentlessly yourself, and that means speaking out. How often do you feel something yet do not express it? In a business meeting, or in a conversation with your partner, your parents, or a friend. Pay attention to how often this occurs. Expressing what you feel is the way to a free and enriched life. This means trusting that whatever comes from a pure heart will work out one way or another.

I often hear people talking about their guilt, when in fact, it is pointless. As Bronnie Ware says: 'Feelings of guilt are toxic.' They serve no purpose. What is behind us, is no more. Wasting your energy on it will get you nowhere. Look back, learn from it, take responsibility, and stay in the present. Even if it seems complicated, letting go of guilt is a choice you make by accepting yourself and forgiving yourself for the things you might have wanted to do differently.

You can see life as a big playground. Do you choose to get back up when you fall, or do you stay on the side-line? Hop into life and please show yourself great compassion for what you have done in the past. No good comes of tormenting yourself with negative thoughts and guilt. You can start every day with a clean slate.

The Symbolism of Your Name

I will end this chapter with a personal story about my name, because this, at its core, is about being who you are and taking up space from your rightful place.

My parents named me Karin at birth. Aged seven, I decided to change my name to Evelien. Something strange happened at school in the period from kindergarten onwards, my teachers seemed to be automatically distorting my name. Carien was even the name that featured on the cover of one of my report cards. I felt very uncomfortable with this as a child and even developed an aversion to this corruption of my name. I would never have chosen Carien, I was born Karin.

One Sunday afternoon, when I was seven years old, good friends of my parents came to visit. I knew them very well and called them uncle and aunt. I talked about this name issue with this uncle. I couldn't help but share with him what happened to my name at school and how I felt about it. At a certain point, he suggested something, namely, to change my name and solve the problem in that way. I thought it was a brilliant solution. We discussed the 'strategy' for the next day when I would go back to school and the plan was forged.

When I walked into the classroom on Monday morning, I immediately told the teacher I had an important announcement to make because I had a new name. The teacher called me forward at the start of the lesson, put a chair down and asked me to stand on it. And so, there I stood, as a seven-year-old girl and told the class that from that day on I wanted to be called Evelien, and it happened. That is how I became Evelien and I patiently stuck to it when people made a mistake. You get older, go to secondary school, and after a while hardly anyone remembers that your official name used to be different.

Years ago, I studied the meaning of my name. My parents chose to call me Karin, the name which still figures on all formal documents. Karin means 'pure', a beautiful meaning that I feel connected to. And will remain connected to, no matter what I choose to be called. My signature is a living proof.

The name Evelien means 'giving life' and for a long time, that is how I saw I was to live my life. Years in which I was not sufficiently true to myself, years searching for myself, for my identity and my soul path. More often than enough I did not take my rightful place and stand up for who I am. I chose jobs that were not always good for me, loves that ultimately were not a good enough match. All these side roads have led to where I am now and every day I remind myself that I am allowed to be relentlessly myself, with respect for others and my environment. Allowing myself to be my authentic self, and that is exactly what my birth name stands for.

I gave my forename some more thought a few years ago and decided that I would continue to call myself Evelien in this life. Apart from all the practical and emotional reasons to do so, there is no doubt in my mind that there is a connection from the heart with the name my parents gave me at birth. I am grateful to them for that and that is what it is all about for me. That is also being true to yourself.

- ∞ There is no space scarcity preventing a human being from taking up his space.
- ∞ To express what you feel, you need to take up space.
- ∞ During the midlife phase, both sexes search for a way to make room for their female sensitive side.
- ∞ To take up space from a connection with your soul you need to:
  - Be aware of your self-sabotaging patterns.
  - Accept and appreciate yourself and dare to make 'mistakes'.
  - Let go of the judgments and opinions of others.
- ∞ Feelings of guilt are pointless. Be compassionate with yourself.

17

BEING GRATEFUL

Allowing a sense of gratitude in your life is a conscious choice. The power of practicing gratitude is huge. Especially when it is gratitude for everything in our lives so far. I would like to share with you how you can work with gratitude, to discover its magical impact on your life and the importance of slowing down, standing still and relaxing while doing so.

Your Way of Slowing Down

To access your feeling of gratitude, you need to slow down. Imagine you fill a glass with sand and water, then put your hand on it and shake it. It is only once you put the glass down and let it rest for a while that the sand will slowly settle, and the water become clear again. This is exactly how it is in life: slowing down and becoming still, leads to clarity and that brings insight.

There are many ways to slow down and find inner peace. Meditation is one way, provided you do it in a way that suits you. Meditation is nothing else than connecting with yourself and staying there, with your truth. It is bringing your thoughts back into the moment when they go astray. Do not try to stop the flow of thoughts by force, it is a question of being with what is. Do not get hung up on the word meditation either. Some people object to it because they do not know how it can work for them, or they give it a meaning that is not in line with the essence of meditation.

When I sit at my pondering place in the early morning, I am alone. Sometimes I close my eyes to turn inward in silence, other times I stare at the garden or immediately start writing. Whatever arises in me is allowed to be there. Sometimes I shine, feel energetic and powerful and sometimes I am moved, feel vulnerable or cry. That moment in the morning, when I feel an intense connection with myself, is sacred to me. It is my me-time and nourishes me throughout the day. I set my intention for the day, which makes me conscious of how I want to feel, then I let go and go about my day.

There are many ways to meditate, you can do it while working in the garden, painting, writing, or doing nothing. In all cases it is more than the one-sided image of sitting in a lotus position on a yoga cushion. What I have found to be most important in meditation is that you do it somewhere nice, where you can be yourself and can sit undisturbed. When you focus your energy and attention on what you are doing in the moment, you arrive at yourself. It is your truth that you feel in the silence with yourself and that brings you into the now.

Slowing down can also mean choosing to stand in the longest queue at the supermarket checkout instead of the shortest. Choose your way of slowing down and start playing with it. Do not let it become a goal in itself, but a way of discovering how it can help you increase your awareness.

I regularly hear people say, 'I am ruled by my agenda,' or 'I feel restless and want more time for myself.' Slowing down helps you to become more aware of your natural rhythm. The value of recognizing and acknowledging the rhythm that suits your nature is great and living accordingly is even greater. What I mean by *rhythm* is knowing, for example, which daily rhythm is best for your body and mind, but also how the different seasons affect you. The trick is to go along with the season's dynamics that suit you. For one person this may mean slowing down and withdrawing in winter and for another it means pulling the plug during the summer to recharge the batteries. Everyone is different in this respect.

In order to discover your natural rhythm, it is important to focus on yourself. This may sound simple, but for many it is not. Women in particular, tend, with the best of intentions, to overshoot the mark in caring for others and in doing so, overlook their own needs. There are of course situations in which you put yourself and your own wishes aside for the sake of the collective, of your loved ones or because of a specific situation. That is what I call humanity, but when this happens structurally at your cost and the cost of your own development, you cross a line that is not good for anyone. Nor is it the idea that you deprive someone else of the chance of taking care of themselves. It is a question of finding the balance between being yourself, living according to your own rhythm and at the same time being involved with others in a healthy way.

Slowing down enables you sometimes to realize that it is not (yet) the right time for an idea, a new job, a new assignment, a new house, or a new relationship. 'You can't do the right thing at the wrong time,' is an old wisdom that says it all. In life it is finding the way to ride the waves and trust that whatever is needed will present itself at the right moment. In the meantime, keep moving, keep playing and exploring, and learn to listen more and more to the whispers of your heart (see chapter thirteen).

When Life Brings You to a Standstill

Some people are caught up in a rhythm which holds them captive and they have little or no idea how to free themselves from it in order to slow down and relax. People who feel like a hamster in a wheel and cannot get out. Sometimes something drastic happens in your life, which forces you to take action, such as the loss of a job or a loved one, or you fall ill. Life literally brings you to a standstill. This is a gift of time as I discussed in chapter twelve. You are offered a sort of timeout to do, or discover, what is meant to be done in it. This harsh lesson is nothing more than a gift to turn inwards and come to the insights needed to move forward in a way that suits who you are. Like Tim:

Tim works as a financial interim manager and has been doing so for years with great but also tough assignments. He lives alone in a beautiful flat in Amsterdam. He is the type who likes taking things on and goes the extra mile. Clients love him. Tim says that his work is his life, that it brings him fulfilment and that he is used to hard work.

While Tim was graduating, his mother suddenly passed away. That was a tough period in his life. He visits his retired father in the South once every two months, more is just not possible. He does speak to him once a week and his father manages reasonably well on his own. He has a social life and that thought makes Tim feel better.

Tim's younger sister lives in Spain with her family. They don't speak often, but they are close. Tim has recently met someone, but he doesn't have much time for her. Their love is still young.

One rainy day in October, Tim was working through the evening to meet a deadline for his new assignment when his phone rang. It was his father's neighbor who had found his father in the kitchen. The ambulance was on its way. Tim immediately left for his parents' house. His father had suffered a stroke.

One thing was sure in the period that followed, he wanted to be there for his father. For the next six months, he commuted to the South every week until his father recovered. Tim felt faced with an enormous dilemma, with a sister at a distance, a father in need of help and a client to whom he was loyal. Recurring flashbacks to the loss of his mother also stirred up a lot of emotions. With a heavy heart, he decided to quit his assignment in order to create space for what was really important to him.

As difficult as it was for Tim due to his conflicting loyalties, he felt this period ended up being the turning point in his life. He resumed his work at some point, but not in the way he had before. He spent more time visiting his father, and on his friends, and his relationship. As intense as this experience was, he was grateful that his father was still there and that he himself had discovered the enrichment of having more balance in his life.

Tim's example is one of many. People do not see the point of slowing down as they are caught in the frenzy of the day.

The familiar is a secure base and determines their thinking and actions.

I trust that the change occurs when someone is ready for it. I have experienced this myself in my life and would not want to go back to the way things were in the past. The inner peace and relaxation I experience in how I live my life now are priceless. I feel that this is the life I was intended to live. Therein lies the crux, to discover your natural rhythm and how you can best come into your own in life from the roots of your 'being'.

Relaxation

Many people only get around to relaxing on weekends or when they are on holiday. The pressure of work, tension or stress caused by their work is such that there is little room for relaxation during the week. Maybe you recognize this? How often do you ask yourself what you actually need? It is precisely at moments of high pressure, when you are more or less ruled by your schedule, that you should ask yourself the question: 'What do I need?'

This question is actually a very simple one, yet so many find it difficult to answer. It has to do with the ability to feel, to stay out of your head and to plumb into your heart and gut feeling (see chapter twelve).

Slowing down and relaxing provides room for inspiration and opens new opportunities. We access our natural energy when we are relaxed, and those around us feel it. That is why you attract what is right for you. That is so much more than knowing what you want or familiarizing yourself with new ideas and convictions through affirmations. It is feeling your energy with every fiber of your being and exhaling it.

It is what you radiate that makes the difference: as inside, so outside. Just look at other people: the look in their eyes, their facial expression, and their voice. It is not always easy to see this in ourselves, but the people around you who know you well can see this flawlessly. For me, for example, it manifests itself in my voice. People who know me well can tell immediately from my voice where I stand, how I am and how my energy is.

Being Grateful

Gratitude can have an immensely powerful effect on your mood. Everyone has days when they are not feeling well or are bothered by something which demands energy and affects the mood. Gratitude is the magic word to turn that around in a fraction of a second. There are always, regardless of your situation, things you can be grateful for, no matter how small and seemingly simple. Even if you are really in a tight spot and struggle to see the light at the end of the tunnel, there are always things you can be grateful for. Think for example of the fact that you have a roof over your head, that you can breathe, that you are alive, that you have friends, that you can enjoy a good book or a nice walk, that you live in freedom, that you can walk or that you can see.

> **Gratitude**
> Write down everything you are grateful for. Note at least fifty points, big or very small.

When you focus on allowing a feeling of gratitude, there is no room for worries and fears. So, give yourself and your energy a shot every now and then by dwelling on the things you are grateful for. The power of this 'natural drug' is enormous. You can, for example make a ritual of it, to reflect, every night before going to bed, on three or five things for which you are grateful. If you want to wake up happy, go to sleep grateful. You can also do this at the beginning of the day, when you got up on the wrong side of bed. See what happens.

Grateful for Loss

It probably is more obvious to be thankful for the beautiful and pleasant things we experience in life. The question is how often you stop to think about it and consciously feel grateful. One step further is to also be grateful for the painful, sad, and traumatic things that have happened in our lives. How double that may seem at first glance. For how can you possibly be grateful for the death of a loved one, for an illness – either yours or of a loved one –, for the loss of a great job or assignment, bankruptcy, divorce, losing a great love, let alone your child? There are numerous examples of situations that are emotionally far, not to say extremely far, from our feeling able to be grateful.

Yet, it is true that an important part of our healing lies in how we deal with it and how we can see the new situation as a starting point. In such a way that we can make room for new moments of joy.

Time is a crucial factor in experiencing the power of gratitude. It is not for nothing that people sometimes say:

'Time heals all wounds.' An assumption that, based on my experience, is partly true, but can also be considered a misconception. Time only works in your favor in processing events if you give it the necessary attention and effort.

With time, you can usually feel more and more gratitude for life's lessons. There are often such strong emotions at play in the moment that you cannot yet see the bigger picture and the lessons that can be learnt from it. First comes a sense of disbelief, apathy and sometimes even denial. It is only sometime later that anger arise, after which, slowly, resignation takes place. How long this takes will depend on the nature of the person involved and on the situation. After acceptance, there is an opening for a new beginning. It is therefore not surprising that radical events often bring about a turning point in a person's life. I will conclude with Anne's story.

Anne had a very bad fall years ago and almost lost her lower leg. She slipped on a wet parking garage floor, and her life literally skidded to a standstill. The impact on her life was immense. She could do nothing at all and that with two young children, a fresh divorce, and her own business. 'I had to slow down. The universe called me to order and it was very much needed.' She explains how grateful she feels when she looks back and how valuable it was that after the accident she discovered her tremendous strength. 'It was not a choice, but being still, reflecting, brought me so much power. I am not so easily scared any more. As long as I can feel my optimism in life, then I am fine.'

- ∞ Slowing down helps you to access your sense of gratitude.
- ∞ Slowing down and relaxing provides room for inspiration and opens new opportunities in your life.
- ∞ Gratitude can have a powerful effect on your mood in the moment and it can be found in the smallest of things.
- ∞ When you focus on feeling gratitude, there is no room for worries and fears.
- ∞ Sometimes life brings you to a standstill, and as difficult as that may be in the moment, trust that there is a reason for it.

PART 5
CONTRIBUTING

18

DISCOVERING YOUR CONTRIBUTION TO THE WHOLE

"The true value of a human being only comes to maturity when he has found his higher destiny and takes his own individual place in the greater whole, with body, mind and soul." – Christina von Dreien

Knowing who you are brings you inner peace. The trick now is to stay true to yourself, and from there, to take up your space and to share what you have to bring to the world. I will help you in this chapter, take a look at who you are in a much broader context, which I call the greater whole. I will stimulate you to think big and investigate how you can best contribute to the greater whole.

We all want to feel satisfied and fulfilled in our (working) life. But what is it inside us that leads to that feeling? Earlier, in chapter three, I talked about joy as the spice of life. Being of significance to the greater whole is closely related, and significantly contributes to it. Instead of losing yourself in worries, fears, and negative thoughts about what is happening in the world, it is better to focus your energy on what you can do to make a positive contribution. This, furthermore, is the way to feed yourself a positive feeling, just think of the bliss I mentioned in chapter fifteen.

The power of change of the collective is the sum of the individual transformations that people go through. As Mahatma Gandhi said: 'Be the change you want to see in the world.' Shake off what is not yours, your burdening ego and the thoughts that can lead and seduce you. Every day that you can see, feel, and radiate your own light to those around you means doing justice to your existence and to what you want to leave behind. By working on increasing your self-awareness, you tap into the driving force of change. All that this requires from you is attention, dedication and trust.

Sometimes it is necessary to first make your world a little smaller in order to eventually have a big impact. I am convinced the world will look very different and the shift that is so needed will take place, once we are all ourselves. Back to basics, to our foundation, in connection with nature. Staying true to our roots is the connection with our soul.

Thinking Big

When it comes to your contribution to the greater whole, it helps to think big. By thinking big, you also learn to put things into perspective and develop more empathy and compassion. What thinking big is, is very personal. Ask ten people what it means to them and you will get ten different answers. It is striking to note that some people find it easier to indicate what it is not, rather than what it is.

I have asked a number of entrepreneurs to share what thinking big means to them, from a personal and business perspective. Here are some of their thoughts for inspiration. Thinking big is:

- Daring to stick your head out and energetically occupy your space, as long as your intentions are pure.
- Being able to get past your own ego.
- Not being afraid to be yourself.
- Having a universal perspective and seeing that your possibilities are unlimited.
- Thinking outside the norms and values that have been held up to us in this earthly reality; and seeing that this is not *the* reality but *a* reality.
- Thinking about the effects of your actions on everything around you, both people and the environment, and acting accordingly.
- Training yourself to take a few steps back when you encounter problems, considering the matter and then arriving at a different solution than what your primary reaction would have been.
- Stepping outside the framework in which you usually do things.
- Setting your own direction.
- Sometimes choosing to leave something behind and accepting it.
- Continuously challenging yourself to become a better person and asking yourself how, in terms of work, partner, and friends.
- Placing everything you do in a larger perspective, allowing new information in and broadening your frame of reference.

- Expanding your view, also geographically.
- Thinking ahead and offering customers solutions, looking at the bigger picture and the ripple effect in the distant future.
- Believing in yourself and not letting yourself be hindered by beliefs you have imposed on yourself or which have been imposed upon you.
- Going not only for the solution you dream of, but also for the one you have not dared dream of.
- Having an antenna to feel whether something is right for you, which differs from knowing from what we have been taught.
- Looking at everything with wonder, then you will see new things, different things and you will gain new insights.

Thinking big is looking, seeing, and feeling beyond the three-dimensional world we live in. Actually, this is the core of my own ability to think big. This is why I resonate with people with whom I feel that the communication and mutual contact go beyond what we say, read and write and what is obvious to most people. It is the magic in the connection with yourself, with others, with nature and with the greater whole that is infinite in its possibilities and makes you hungry to discover more about life and what it is really all about. In my eyes, that is more than living within your own backyard. The fact that I can feel that in every fiber of my body is an enormous enrichment. For me this is also a one-way street, there is no going back to ignorance.

Thinking big sounds nice, but what does it actually mean to you? Stop and think about it by doing the following exercise.

What is Thinking Big?
1. What does 'thinking big' mean to you? What is it about? Think about it in both a business and private context.
2. In how far do you consider yourself a big – in the sense of broad – thinker?
3. Where do you still let yourself be limited from thinking even bigger?
4. What do you need in order to think even bigger?

Collective Role

We are beings of flesh and blood, born into a human body that is 'inhabited' by our souls. The fact that we enter this world alone at birth and die alone does not mean that we are not part of a greater whole. We are so much more than a mortal body in this one existence on earth.

All Is One
You have probably heard the saying: 'All is one' before. I used to wonder about its deeper meaning and for a long time I was unable to grasp what it is really about. The time was not yet ripe to grasp and feel this principle. Until I came to even deeper levels of the core of my being. That is to say, was able to distinguish between my earthly personality on the one hand and the roles I assume with it, and on the other, knowing and feeling my soul and why I am in this life.

> For me, the essence of 'all is one' lies in the realization that everything is connected and that everything is energy, with no beginning and no end. This means that when you take good care of yourself, you take good care of others and everything around you. I use 'taking good care of yourself' in the broadest sense of the word. That is, by allowing yourself to be relentlessly yourself out of love and respect for everything around you and to take up your space.

We are all here on a unique journey, with as individual task to create clarity along the way. We do this by truly embracing life and being relentlessly ourselves. This means discovering our authentic power of being, recognizing and acknowledging our unique gifts and talents, and giving them form and substance. It means having the courage to take our place in life, exactly as intended for each of us.

Your authentic power of being is at the same time part of the collective role we all play and that is your contribution to the greater whole. First, you have turned your attention to your authentic self. You can trust that everything that derives from it, is good, also for the collective. This brings you to the core of your 'being' and from there, you can surrender to all that derives from it.

The only real contribution you make to the greater whole is to rid yourself of everything that does not belong to your *nature* (see chapter four). You then come to the essence of your unique being and your unique gift. What remains then is pure, authentic, unique, and loving, established on a sense of trust and strength. After all, trust and power come from purity and therein lie the basic ingredients for being meaningful to others.

Every day that you can see, feel, and radiate your authentic power of being to those around you, means doing justice to your existence and to what you want to leave behind. By working on increasing your self-awareness, you tap into the driving force of change.

"We travel the endless corridors of our mind, until one day we find a pathway that leads to our own heart. Who you really are has nothing to do with your personality, with what you achieve, your successes, your failures. The you that you think you are, is an actor playing a role chosen by the soul. Your real being is your soul, light without beginning without end. You are an eternal spark of pure creativity with unlimited potential, yearning for expression and fulfilment. Your potential is your destination, and it is waiting for your summons. Trust your heart and make your love and your wisdom available to everything and everyone. In this way, everything you do or make will be a true expression of your soul."
– Toni Carmine Salerno

If you are still asking yourself: 'What do I *really* want? What is my purpose in life?' or 'How can I be of meaning?' then take a step back and focus on gaining inner clarity. I talked about this extensively in Part 4. It is touching your very essence, fully recognizing who you are and loving yourself and acting from there. When you do that, the path will become clear and you can trust that everything that comes out of it is good, also for the collective.

> **Your Contribution**
> Reflect on how you see your role or contribution to the greater whole. You can do this by writing, drawing, painting, or speaking it out loud.
> Then share this with a good sparring partner and see if you make it even clearer.

Humility

Being part of a greater whole means being aware that you are not alone in the world and that you are a cog in a greater whole. This calls for humility, which by no means signifies being subservient or irrelevant. I briefly discussed *empowered humility* in chapter nine on success and ego, here I look at humility in the context of your contribution to the greater whole.

People sometimes say: 'It is not about you.' I would like to nuance that somewhat. After all, you can look at that statement from different angles. It is fundamentally about who you are, but who you are in essence, moving beyond your personality. Your soul is here on Earth in a human body in order to learn something, to develop and from there to establish something, whatever that may be.

Basically, in order to see the bigger picture and gain insight into your role and contribution, you will first have to find yourself. This in fact means first making your world a little smaller by turning your gaze inwards, in order to then be able to take up your space and have an impact on the greater whole. Everyone counts and has something to do here, all the seeds we plant as humans are essential.

Being able to show humility is one thing, but actually

feeling it from within is another. This includes being genuinely grateful for everything in your life and knowing no egotism or self-centeredness. By this I mean in particular, being averse to the use of power and of claiming credit and taking responsibility for caring for yourself. This implies that you can of course think of yourself, but without attaching much value to appropriating things that do not really matter. It is about on the one hand being able to see, feel and appreciate the greatness of the earthly, and on the other, discovering that the pursuit of always wanting more, does not actually bring fulfilment.

Life's magic lies in knowing how to tune in to a feeling of trust and drawing on your own source of energy. Knowing and experiencing that true happiness sits in the simplicity of joy, and that this is a feeling that you can only create from within.

The 16th century English ecclesiast, scholar and writer Robert Burton said: 'Some people are proud of their humility.' A quote that shows how complicated humbleness or humility really is. Do not let it become an end in itself but take to heart what it is all about and challenge yourself to be humble more often for the sake of the greater good. Take a step back and look, from a higher perspective, at yourself and how you live your life.

- ∞ In order to see the bigger picture and gain insight into your role and contribution, you must first find and discover yourself.
- ∞ Your authentic power of being constitutes also part of the collective role that we have and is your contribution to the greater whole.

- ∞ If you are wondering what your purpose in life is, start by focusing on being your authentic self and trust that everything that arises from there is good, also for the collective.
- ∞ Being part of a greater whole means being aware you are a cog in a greater whole. This calls for humility.
- ∞ Everyone counts and has something to do here, all the seeds we plant as humans are essential.

19

DRAFTING YOUR PERSONAL MANIFESTO

A personal manifesto conveys the core of who you are, what drives you in life and why. You can draw the short statements for the manifesto from your self-reflection on the multitude of topics covered in the previous chapters. Everything comes together in the manifesto. Your personal manifesto is a beautiful way to capture who you essentially are, your life purpose, and how you are driven by your deepest desires.

Starting Point

The previous chapter ended by taking a step back and looking at yourself and your soul's mission here on Earth from a helicopter view. This is the starting point to arrive at your own manifesto. You will notice that, if it is the right thing for you now, it will more or less flow effortlessly from your pen or brush. Should you feel resistance, then accept that now is not the right time for it and first focus on other things that will bring you more clarity and focus. Everything in its own time and at its own pace.

I shall share, for inspiration, an example of a personal manifesto. It is my manifesto and therefore not *the* only way to do it, but *a* way of doing it. The reason I am sharing it, is not to make a one-to-one translation of each paragraph to your own situation. The power is in reading it, putting it aside and then, when the time is right, filling in your personal manifesto, in your own unique way.

My Example of a Manifesto

I believe that every person on Earth is on a journey of discovery to get to the core of who he is as a soul in a human body, that is the core of your 'being'.

We are here from a deep longing for love, connection, and fulfilment. I believe that the way to get there starts with self-love, by recognizing and acknowledging the 'divine' in ourselves, our soul. That requires you to expose the rough diamond within and be relentlessly yourself, pure, authentic and sincere, and with compassion for everything and everyone around you.

In my world many people are searching, for their happiness, their roots, and their unique creative power. In my world, people are in a hurry, often have little sincere attention for each other.

I am on Earth to inspire and encourage others to mobilize from a place of purity, love and light. So that they get to see themselves for who they truly are and from there stand up tall and spread their wings, thereby contributing to the world in which we live.

To do this I am loving, gentle and patient with myself. I listen to my inner voice, act on it, and follow my natural rhythm.

I literally stand in the light, indulge in nature, especially the sun and the sea.

I surround myself with people who are loving and sensitive and with whom I can connect on a soul level. People with whom I feel enough room to be me, who encourage me to develop in this life so that I can fulfill my societal mission. I am and will remain true to myself because I know that in this way, I can make my contribution exactly as is intended for me, on this soul mission on Earth.

Drafting Your Own Manifesto

Some people enjoy writing a manifesto in words, while others are more comfortable with a visual format. The power of the manifesto is that it shows your unique character, and this is reflected in both the content and the form. You are completely free to fill it in, in whichever way suits you.

There are questions you can use as guidelines when writing your manifesto. You will find them in the exercise below. If you choose not to answer certain questions, that is fine. The order also in which you choose to include each element in your manifesto, is entirely up to you.

Before you begin answering the questions, it is a good idea to think about the format that you would like to use, and which suits you best. If you choose for a more visually expressive form, such as drawing or painting, then keywords for each question might be a good place to start.

> **Drafting your manifesto**
> 1. What do you stand for in life?
> 2. How do you see the world?

3. What are you accountable for?
4. What are your core values?
5. When do you feel deeply fulfilled?
6. What do you want to signify in life and why is that?
7. Where are you headed and what do you want to leave behind?
8. Who do you want to be?
9. What dreams do you have?
10. What kind of people do you like to be surrounded by?

You may at times not revisit your manifesto for a year and at other moments possibly work on it several times a year to make it fit even better as you get closer to yourself. Life is a great journey of self-discovery and your learning process is never-ending. That is exactly why a personal manifesto moves with you.

Although a manifesto touches on the essence of who you are, drafting it is not a one-off exercise. You are on a lifelong journey of discovery, taking you to the core of who you are. Everything you experience brings you to a deeper level of awareness and understanding of who you are, how you view life, where you are going and why. It is the evolution of your development and it is not cast in stone. If you choose to take inspired action, to learn, to dare and to do, then you will need to recalibrate your manifesto more often than if you do not.

I printed my manifesto in colors, with a fancy font and put it in a nice frame. It has a central place in my office. The fact that it is in my cupboard, right next to my desk, is enough for me. Every now and then, I take it out to absorb the words, to muse about them and to reflect on what I consider to be the essence. This is not really necessary as the content comes from my heart and soul and is part of me. But it enables me to check whether this is still in line with how I experience it.

You do not need to cram into your head what you have worked out in your manifesto. Just like with an authentic story or a good pitch, it is about feeling your message with every fiber of your being and communicating and radiating it. The latter is important; that your story is true and in line with what your body language and expression are telling you deep inside. You cannot have one without the other and even more so, if what you emit does not match what you are sharing, there will be no resonance. You can feel it, especially in interaction with others.

Benchmark for Decisions

Your personal manifesto serves as a benchmark for the decisions you make, also in a business context. It can help you avoid making decisions that are not purely inspired by who you are and what drives you. You have read more, in chapter thirteen, about making choices, especially heartfelt choices. Making the 'wrong' decisions on important matters can have a major impact on your life. Think, for example, of choosing a cooperation partner who does not match your soul mission and development path. Collaborations usually arise from a good idea or from a momentum in the connection between people. At first there is a lot of enthusiasm and energy, and before you know it, you step in and start working together. This usually goes well for a while or sometimes even for years, until you reach a point where you feel that something is just not right. It might start with points of irritation in the cooperation. You try to make the best of it, until you notice that the partner's dreams and personal development paths no longer complement and strengthen each other, but rather get in each other's way. This leads to an impasse. This is exactly when having a personal manifesto is helpful. The pinnacle of each cooperation is the outcome of the individual development of each of the partners concerned.

A personal manifesto helps remind you, in difficult situations such as a deadlocked business partnership, of who you are and what you stand for. There are sometimes circumstances when you just keep going because there is so much that needs to be done, while silently asking yourself what on earth you are doing. When slowing down in these situations, it is useful to have a manifesto. It makes you alert, and if the manifesto is in perfect alignment, you can draw strength from it, immediately recharging your energy so you can put yourself back on the path that is right for you.

Your personal manifesto serves as an anchor in your life and in everything that comes with it, such as your work and the connections you make, both in the private and professional spheres. It reminds you of the source of your being and is the foundation of everything you put out into the world. The intentions that you make and state in your personal manifesto are powerful and strongly impact your own energy. They set things in motion and motion always leads to something better.

MY BIOGRAPHY

I was born in 1971 in Stad Delden, a beautiful place in a wooded area in the east of the Netherlands. I was the youngest in the family, with one older brother. I went to a small Christian primary school of which I have fond memories. A relatively carefree time in which I enjoyed myself with friends and classmates. My parents met in a laboratory in the western part of the country. After my father obtained his doctorate, he got a job in the east of the country and so they settled there a few years before my brother and I were born.

I finished high school aged seventeen and went to the United States for a year where I lived with a family in Oklahoma City. This was an amazing year in which I completely immersed myself in life, culture, school, and sports. I made new friends and thoroughly enjoyed the life I built there from the very beginning. I am still to this day in contact with the family where I stayed. Unfortunately, two dear friends from that period passed away at a young age, which has had a great impact on me. The memories I made that year are etched in my memory and I am grateful for this experience.

Once back in the Netherlands, I studied Business Communication at the Academy for Journalism, settled in Zwolle and a few years later in Utrecht. I then obtained my doctoral degree at the VU (Free University) of Amsterdam, majoring in Culture, Organization & Management. I wanted to gain as much experience as possible during my studies,

and travel. I did internships on Bonaire and in Philadelphia (US) and worked several days a week in a gym as an aerobics and fitness instructor. I was adventurous, but also committed to graduating. I wanted to see more of the world alongside my studies during my last year of university.
I can still remember slipping out of my student house at dawn one Saturday morning. I had hardly told a soul as I set off for Schiphol Airport to apply for a job as a stewardess. I came back with a contract and the world was at my feet. For the next three quarters of a year, I flew around the world: Europe, North, Central and South America and Asia. It was a fantastic but also a strenuous time, during which I learned to work hard alongside my studies, sometimes at impossible hours, and most of all, I learned what resilience is all about.

In 1996, I started my first office job at KLM, as Communication Manager in Engineering & Maintenance. I then continued my career in the field of communication and change management and management development. I did not stay with an organization for much longer than three and a half years. I was constantly looking for new challenges and driven to develop myself further in different branches.

I moved to Utrecht with my partner of the time, and a year later my daughter Julia was born. Apart from the physical ordeal and the change it brought to my life, her birth was above all an intensely loving and special event. I worked practically full-time and had to find a way to best combine my job with motherhood.

In 2005 my daughter, Maud, was born, a second daughter, another extraordinary event. Especially as I had dreamt of having a sister when I was a child. After that, things started changing. I lost my fixed job and decided to continue as an independent entrepreneur. I started working as an interim manager for the tax authorities, ING, Vitens and Philips, among others. At the beginning of 2012, my then partner and I separated, this was a difficult period. I continued as a single parent, albeit in co-parenting. This allowed both their father and I to maintain a close relationship with our daughters, which felt good and was important to all of us.

My love life has been quite turbulent and marked by a quest, above all, for myself. There has always been a longing for love, equality, and a deep connection. And the latter not only in love, but also in friendships that I have come to cherish more and more over the years.

In terms of work, I ended my interim period after about nine years more or less overnight when my then-boyfriend was told early 2015 that he was seriously ill. The report of cancer hit us both like a bomb. I immediately knew that this was my wake-up call. I had not been feeling fulfilled in my work for some time now, so the decision to change course did not come entirely out of the blue. I wanted space to determine my own rhythm and follow my heart. For me, that meant more depth and meaning in my work and, from a business point of view, devoting myself completely to helping people develop, both in their business or job, as in their life.

Hence, I took the plunge and early 2015 started working as a business coach. I set to work with a clean slate, hired a coach and also participated in a year-long program with another coach. I invested heavily in my own development and before I knew it, I had my first clients with whom

I did in-depth one-on-one sessions. Group training sessions followed rapidly and at the end of 2016 I hosted my first own live event for entrepreneurs and entrepreneurial professionals. It was a great time where I learned a lot.

My life is intense and experience-wise, far from monotonous. At times I have wondered where life's user's manual was. Then, little by little, I discovered that the connection with my soul, with my 'being', is the greatest guide I could have in my life. For me, that is about having the courage to be relentlessly myself. My spiritual development became one of the greatest sources of enrichment in my life.

So long as I can develop and have new experiences, I feel that I am alive. Having said that, I feel that should this movement stop, then this would signify the end of my life, but that moment is still far ahead.

Today, as an international speaker, mentor, and business coach, I work with entrepreneurs and professionals who feel stuck and want to take concrete steps forward. These are often people who are in their midlife phase. In 2018, I rolled out my coaching method Signature 4 Success® (www.signature4success.com) and became a mentor for career and business coaches. It is my dream to further expand, in the coming years, my activities internationally. After all the themes that really matter in life, are universal.

AFTERWORD

This is an everlasting journey, which does not end after today. I hope you have enjoyed the inspiration, the stories, and the tools that I have lovingly shared with you. It is now up to you to accept the invitation to take on life and to be relentlessly yourself, with love, surrender and trust. May the encouragement I offer you in this book be a nudge in the right direction to get even closer to your true self.

I am profoundly grateful for the time I have been given to work on this book. It has been a wonderful and intense process of introspection and reflection in which I have sought out peace and quiet, and occasionally the connection with special people in my life. I enjoyed the walks, the conversations, and the valuable musings. Each conversation and encounter was unique, honest and true. There are a few people in particular I would like to single out in my thanks. Tracy for your big heart, friendship, and support from a distance. Anne for your unconventional-thinking, sparring and friendship. I also thank Frank, Femke, Mirjam, RJ, Dieta, Wietze, Julie, Willem, David, Maria, Esther, and Karina. Arjen Snijder for the layout of the cover, Herman Chow for the photography and Julie Kennedy for the translation. Thanks also to Dominick Domasky and his team for the final editing and the interior design. I would also like to thank Bauke for his loving support in the last phase of the realization of this book.

There are so many more who have inspired me on my life's path with their stories and thoughts. All of this has contributed to the maturing of my insights and the realization of this book. Last but not least, I thank my parents for their unceasing and inexhaustible love, and for the magical fact that they have given me this life.

I dedicate this book to my two beautiful daughters Julia and Maud. I love you with all my heart and am grateful for the life lessons you teach me every day.

"Eyes are blind, you have to look with the heart. For your heart leads the way to your soul."
– Antoine de Saint-Exupéry

REFERENCES

Books

- Antoine de Saint-Exupéry, *De kleine prins* [The Little Prince], Ad Donker, 1989.
- Barbara Hand Clow, *Liquid Light of Sex; Kundalini Rising at Mid-Life Crisis*, Bear & Company, 1996.
- Bernadette von Dreien, *Christina – tweeling als licht geboren. Deel 1* [Twins Born as Light, Book 1], Uitgeverij Akasha, 2019.
- Bernadette von Dreien, *Christina – het visioen over het goede, Deel 2* [The Vision of the Good, Book 2], Uitgeverij Akasha, 2020.
- Bronnie Ware, *The Top Five Regrets of the Dying, A Life Transformed by the Dearly Departing*, Hay House, 2012.
- Christiane Beerlandt, *De sleutel tot zelfbevrijding, Levensfilosofie voor een gelukkig en gezond bestaan,* Encyclopedie van de Psychosomatiek, [The Key to Self-Liberation, The Philosophie for a Happy and Healthy Existence, Encyclopedia of Psychosomatics], Beerlandt Publications, 1993-2018.
- Christina von Dreien, *Christina – bewustzijn schept vrede, Deel 3* [Consciousness Creates Peace, Book 3], Uitgeverij Akasha, 2019.
- Dalai Lama, Desmond Tutu en Douglas Abrams, *The Book of Joy*, Hutchinson, 2016.
- Eckhart Tolle, *Een nieuwe aarde, De uitdaging van deze tijd* [A New Earth, Create a Better Life], Ankh Hermes, 2017.
- George Kohlrieser, *Hostage at the Table*, Jossey-Bass, 2006.
- Inayat Khan, *Het doel van het leven* [The Purpose of Life],

Servire, 1985.
- Jed McKenna, *Spirituele verlichting? Vergeet het maar!* [Spiritual Enlightenment, The Damnedest Thing], Samsara, 2016.
- Johanna Maria Riemen, Sophie R. Jacobsen, *Een sleutel ... om het slot te openen*, 2019.
- Pamela Kribbe, *Bezield leven* [Heart Centered Living], Altamira, 2019.
- Pamela Kribbe, *De verboden vrouw spreekt* [The Forbidden Female Speaks], Altamira, 2020.
- Stella Bergsma, *Nouveau Fuck, manifest*, Nijgh & Van Ditmar, 2020.
- Thich Nhat Hanh, *You Are Here*, Shambhala, 2009.

Additional sources of inspiration
- Abraham Hicks
- Abu Sa'id
- Alan Watts
- Brené Brown
- Brihadaranyaka Unpanishad
- Boeddha
- Camille Pissarro
- Deepak Chopra
- Elisabeth Kübler-Ross
- Eric Berne
- George Bernard Shaw
- Gert Gigerenzer
- Gregg Braden
- Guy Winch
- Jackie Freemantle a.k.a Nobela
- Jan Geurtz

- Jay Shetty
- Jim Whittaker
- Khalil Gibran
- Mahatma Gandhi
- Matt Kahn
- Paulo Coelho
- Prince Ea
- Robert Burton
- Rumi
- Stephen Covey Senior
- Steven Pont
- Toni Carmine Salerno
- Wayne Dyer

www.ingramcontent.com/pod-product-compliance
Lightning Source LLC
Chambersburg PA
CBHW071335080526
44587CB00017B/2842